ALONG THE LONG, LONG, TRAIL

ALONG THE LONG, LONG TRAIL

A private soldier's experiences on the SOMME. (Dedicated to the pals whose names are inscribed on the THIEPVAL memorial to the missing besides those who sleep beneath the simple headstones).

by

Arthur Wilson
- Sarg. (391104)

Published by
Longhirst Press

First published 2006
by
Longhirst Press

Sterling House
Brunswick Industrial Estate
Wideopen
Newcastle upon Tyne
NE13 7BA

Printed by
City Printing Works Ltd.
Chester-le-Street

British Library Cataloguing-in-Publication Data

A catalogue record of this book is available
from the British Library

ISBN

0 946978 05 0

Prologue

THE SHEFFIELD PALS BATTALION

When Britain declared war on Germany on 4 August 1914, its army consisted of some 450,000 men, supported by 250,000 reservists. Even though confidence was high enough for people to predict that the war would be over by Christmas, it was clear that the country's professional army did not have enough manpower to take on the enemy's large armies, swelled through conscription.

Lord Kitchener, Secretary of State for War, realised this but he had to face the problem of conscription in the UK being politically unacceptable in 1914. His response was to raise a New Army, manned entirely by volunteers.

A few days later, Kitchener's famous "Your Country needs You" poster was issued. At the same time, General Sir Henry Rawlinson proposed that recruitment would be more effective if men could form battalions made up of people from the same location. The first four Pals battalions were raised in Liverpool by Lord Derby. Nationwide, around 30,000 men were enlisting every day by the end of August. By the end of the year, Kitchener's New Army totalled a million men.

The rush to join was fuelled by a number of factors. There was optimism that the war would be over by Christmas and many did not want to miss the challenge. There was much peer pressure, not to mention those women who pressed white feathers indiscriminately on young men not in uniform. Army service also presented an escape from poverty for some.

The proposal for a Sheffield battalion came from the Duke of Norfolk and Sir George Franklin of the University of Sheffield. Its initial full title was "The Sheffield University and City Special Battalion of the York and Lancaster Regiment".

Over 1,400 men were recruited. There was a high proportion of professional and blue-collar men so that, by the end of the war, some 500 of these original volunteers had been commissioned. The first parade took place at Norfolk Barracks, Sheffield. Around three hundred men failed the medical examination. A further fifty were rejected on the grounds that their civilian work was essential to the war effort. This was not surprising in a city like Sheffield, the home to such engineering giants as Vickers.

Meanwhile, the regular and territorial armies were also recruiting. The Sheffield Territorial regiment, the Hallamshires, was notably popular, which explains why the city had just one Pals battalion. Inevitably, all this led to a shortage of experienced officers. Some came out of retirement, others were brought home from India. Initial training took place at Redmires, Ripon and on Salisbury Plain.

At first, the battalion was placed in 115th Infantry Brigade, part of the 5th New Army. This was later re-numbered 94th and placed in 31st Division, 4th Army.

On 21 December 1915, the battalion embarked on the Blue Funnel Line HMT Nestor at Devonport, arriving at Alexandria on 1 January 1916.

The battalion's task in Egypt was to strengthen the Canal's defences against a possible attack by Turkey. When it became clear that the Turkish threat was not likely to materialise, the battalion embarked on HMT Briton at Port Said on 10 March and arrived in Marseilles five days later. Eighteen days later, it arrived at the front line in northern France.

The battalion was located in the Colincamps sector, facing its objective, the village of Serre.

The series of attacks which became known as the Battle of the Somme was mounted at the request of the French, who had come under immense pressure at Verdun. The task of 31st Division was to provide a defensive flank for the reminder of 4th Army, which was to attack the German front line system. In order to form this flank, the division had first to capture the village of Serre. This was the task of 93rd and 94th brigades.

After the war, it became known that careless talk in England had given the Germans a very precise picture of what was about to happen, and when. Furthermore, British intentions would have become clear from the bombardment which began on 24 June and which intensified over the next few days. Rains cause a two day delay beyond the original date set for the attack – giving the Germans yet more time to brace themselves – and the men went over the top on the morning of 1 July.

The first day of the Battle of the Somme resulted in 60,000 British casualties and so became the darkest day in the history of the British Army.

A few British soldiers reached Serre, covering the 700 yards by ten in the evening, but at a high price. The German lines had survived the bombardment and their machine gunners had easy targets in the lines of advancing men. Of the 651 men of the Sheffield Pals who set out that morning, 512 were killed in action, missing in action, died of wounds or were taken prisoner, a 79 per cent casualty rate.

PREFACE

by Stuart Wilson

Arthur Wilson, my father, was born in Rotherham in April 1894 and was educated at Rotherham Grammar School. He was a junior reporter with the Sheffield Independent at the outbreak of war when he enlisted with the Sheffield City Pals Battalion. He served with them until he was wounded on 1 July 1916.

On his recovery he was transferred to the Northumberland Fusiliers, with whom he served until the end of the War. He was mentioned in the Despatch of General Frederick Lambart, Earl of Cavan, of 26 October 1918. After the war he rejoined the staff of the Sheffield Independent and was appointed Deputy Chief Reporter in 1922 and Chief Reporter in 1926. In 1937 he became Editor and held that position until the newspaper was taken over and closed the following year.

He then transferred to Newcastle upon Tyne as News Editor of the Newcastle Chronicle and was no doubt able to renew friendships with old comrades from the Northumberland Fusiliers. He remained in Newcastle until his death in 1964.

Reporters who received their early training on his staff include Sir Denis Hamilton, Olga Franklin, Brian Redhead, Harold Williamson, George House and John Robson.

He was married to Kathleen, his "vision" during the War, from 1923 until her death in 1932. He married Gertrude in 1934 and together they had two children.

I have gathered from papers he left that he visited the battlefields many times in the 1920's and once with a fellow Pals survivor in 1938 after the closure of the Sheffield Independent.

I have no recollection of him ever mentioning the 1914-1918 War. The manuscript of this book was not discovered until more than ten years after his death.

CHAPTER 1

Only the gentle lap-lap of the almost placid waters of the Suez Canal broke the soft stillness of an Eastern night. Overhead, the stars shone brilliantly, as they do on a frosty night in England or from the velvet of a tropical sky. Occasionally, the wonderful stillness was broken by a slight plop as a water rat dived back into the depths of the canal. Away to the south, many miles away, gleamed a steady light. It was the only sign of life - the searchlight of a distant steamer such as all boats on the canal had to carry by night.

A keen observer might have seen, silhouetted on the top of the Eastern bank of the canal, the form of a soldier, with sun helmet and equipment. He might even have seen by his side the end of his rifle barrel; might occasionally have caught a glimpse of the fixed bayonet. Had he been closer he would have seen that the soldier was staring hard to the East, away out into the distant night and loneliness of the desert. He was on guard, and about his feet were two others; his relief, slumbering heavily, for they had travelled six miles to this post along the mud-caked bank of the canal, baked hard and rough since it left the dredgers.

Had there been any real danger of an approaching enemy, these three were in a precarious position, for the nearest bridge across the canal was six miles away, and they were three miles from their colleagues at the next post. It was January 1916, and these young soldiers, fresh from England, had simply been told off to this duty, knowing very little of what to expect. Had they known it, there was no enemy unless it might have been a marauding band, within a hundred miles. But this young sentry - he could have been no more than 21 - had no idea of this. All he knew was that the safety of his comrades might depend on his alertness.

Even then, he could not forbear an occasional glance to the left along the silver band of the canal, for away there in the distance gleamed the North Star and it was away over there, 3,000 miles off that home lay. And it was away over there, so far away that a girl, a girl who though he scarcely know her, had become all the world to him. He had only met her a few weeks before the outbreak of war. Possible he had not spoken to her a dozen times before, in the September of 1914, he had answered the call and enlisted to aid his country.

But those were electric days when boys' emotions were fired quickly. He had known within the space of weeks what in ordinary times it might have taken a man months

9

to learn - that this girl was the one girl in his life. Wherever he might go, in whatever circumstances, hers would always be the image in his heart.

Already he had dreamed of her hundreds of times as he had stood as he stood now, with rifle and bayonet ready. As he had tramped backwards and forwards listening to the sweet chimes of Ripon Cathedral he had conjured up visions of that beautiful girl. Bleak winter nights on Salisbury Plain had been warmed by reflections on the never-to-be-forgotten but rare meetings.

The Sunday afternoon when she had consented to take the second turning instead of the first on the way home. The glimpses he had caught of her fleeting figure as he marched away to camp. The wonderful day out on the moorlands. True there was a party, but he had managed to keep her to himself most of the day. Towards the end she had tired and it was his privilege to take her yielding, soft arm in order to help her along. He could feel that arm, could scent her sweet fragrance tonight as he gazed into the desert.

There were other occasions equally sweet, and finally that unbelievable night when she had allowed him to take her into his arms and had assented to his faltering request that she would wait for him.

On many a night like this he had recalled that scene - every action, every word. Scores of times he had weighed each phrase over in his mind and wondered, did she mean it as he had meant it? And had he been fair to ask such a question of a young girl? He was a soldier now and every day brought more news to show what a grim business he had entered.

Thousands of men who had enlisted when he did had been killed before this. Thousands more had been maimed. Could he make her a widow before she had been married? Could he expect her to take him if he were injured? He knew he could not. A hundred times he had decided to write and tell her she need trouble no further about the promise; but he could not bring himself to do it. He could not face the future without that vision. It had become part of his soul. He knew that, come what may, that girl would always be his sheet anchor. Even if she did not wait - and he could not blame her if she did not, he knew in his inmost heart that there would be no other woman for him.

Again was it fair when he had no prospects? But for the events of six years ago it might have been all right. Then he had a good home. His father was apparently a successful businessman. He himself had been booked for a university career, but disaster had come. The flourishing business was not flourishing at all, and it had faded away like a smoke cloud, leaving a wreckage of unsettled debts. With a courage and determination far beyond his years he had resolved then that some day he would make himself responsible for that wreckage.

But despite his utmost efforts he had as yet achieved nothing. To all intents and purposes he was penniless. And what were the prospects of the future, even if this war business were over? This job was safe, he believed, but what was it?

In those days newspaper work was a poorly paid business. What chance of building up a home on the earnings of a pressman? Yet others had done it. But was it fair to expect a girl who obviously had been gently nurtured to share that struggle with him?

The night drew on. He glanced at his watch. It would soon be time to arouse his relief. He glanced again to the north. Never before had that bleak star seemed so friendly. And he offered up a prayer to the God who made the stars that his beloved one should be happy and free from the worries of the war.

Had he but known, he was to offer up that prayer on countless more nights as he stood on the parapet; gazing East at the German trenches on the Somme, gazing North, South and East on the Salient, and again across the snow swept peaks of the Assago Plateau, before at last he would get the opportunity of asking that girl if she really had meant it when she promised to wait.

But for all those months, months which were to stretch into years, that girl's face was to shine before him, a beacon and sheet anchor to help him through the greatest trials a man has ever been called upon to bear. Could he have borne the separation so long had he known it? It is a kind providence which hides such things from us.

Nor was he alone. It was the distant vision of a true, pure girl that carried many a man through the bitter sorrow and trials of the war.

Wherever they were, these lads bore bravely up, hoping against hope that eventually they would come through; praying continually both that those girls would care and at the same time that they would not worry, and praying that eventually there would be a happy meeting.

It was four by the gunmetal watch our sentry tugged from his tunic pocket. Reluctantly he dragged his mind back to the present and roused the youth at his feet. "Your turn Ern", he said as he jerked the other vigorously. Grumbling and blessing the war, the other rolls over and staggers unsteadily to his feet.

"Just dreaming of home" he said. "Don't you wish we were there, Jack?"

Jack North did not reply. His feelings just then were too deep for words. Instead he pulled his heavy coat about him and prepared to make himself comfortable in the bottom of the trench. Soon he was fast asleep, dreaming of home and her.

Two hours later the two sleeping forms were aroused by Ern's sharp "Who goes there?" "Westminster Bridge" came the reply. "Pass friend" said Ern.

It was the sergeant with the northern patrol and the seven of them were soon on their way back on the six miles tramp to the ferry.

This canal patrol lasted three weeks when one day the news filtered through that the company was to join the battalion to move out for desert duty.

The march began at two o'clock one morning. It is a horrible hour to begin a march, but in the desert marches must begin early for it is impossible to march in the heat of the day.

In the very early morning no matter what time he may have retired, a soldier feels, in his own parlance, like nothing on earth. His feet will not obey him. He stumbles over things that are not there. He kicks the feet of the man in front. His own feet are kicked by the man behind. He staggers and flounders into the man next to him. Tempers are frayed and generally, it is not a pleasant business.

The battalion marched due east, for nearly four hours when suddenly the sky was illuminated with a wonderful red light. Quickly the most glorious colours chased each other across the firmament. The weary soldiers forgot their grumbles in the glory of the heavens. Each one kept his gaze expectantly ahead and in a few minutes a great globe shot up - it was sunrise.

On they marched. At first the sun was welcome for it warmed and relieved night-stiffened joints. But soon its powers became such that perspiration poured down the tanned faces of the men. Each man swung doggedly along, his eyes fastened on the sweating neck of the man in front.

Straps chafed the shoulders and hips. Rifles got heavier. A wind sprang up, driving the biting sand into their faces. Eyes, ears and mouths were choked with sand. It found its way through puttees into boots, rasping like sandpaper against hot, tender feet.

"Oh for a cup of tea at Rugeley cafe" choked Ern. "Don't mention it" spat out the perspiring Jack. "Do you remember the tea in the cafe at Rugeley?" "Shut up!" urged another. "Keep the home fires burning" yelled another and soon a thousand voices were yelling derisively the song they had sung in the snows of Salisbury Plain. They were soon tired of singing and the column straggled on.

It said much for the long training in England that not a man fell out. They were, in fact, a fine body of men. Very few were over thirty. The majority were in their early Twenties - fine, big strapping fellows who had responded to the rigorous training and become fit, hardened men. Mostly they were young professional men. The majority had tramped the moors for pleasure, long before they had marched them for training. But there is a vast difference between a ramble and a march. Only months of training had fitted them to carry packs across the desert. But they were young and proud of their strength and only the direst need would have made them betray the honour of the battalion by falling out.

At last a group of gleaming tents came into sight and, by mid-day, they were squatting about, sheltered from the blazing sun in double skin tents and drinking the much-prized drop of water that was issued as a special concession for the march.

There followed some arduous days of work. Strong points of trenches had to be dug and revetted and wire entanglements had to be placed in front of them. They did not know it but a great man had been out here since the last attack on the canal by the Turks and Kitchener had ordered that the next attack must be met in the desert to avoid damage to the precious canal.

It was here that Jack was to learn what at a later date was to introduce him to one of the most dangerous jobs on the Western Front. He and another Slayford friend, Jim Foggitt, were told off specially to learn wiring. Working barbed wire is indeed an art, if it is not to be a torture and many a time Jack wondered what would have happened to his hands if he had been given this work immediately on leaving his office job. A rifle had been bad enough, as many split knuckles testified but barbed wire would have been torture.

But even barbed wire can be tamed and Jack soon discovered that he was quite an adept at twisting this treacherous stuff into all the different shapes that modern warfare demands. Most wonderful of all, He could do it without scratching himself.

Time wore on. It was not at all an unpleasant job if only there had been more water, but the whole supply had to be brought out by camel and the result was a ration of only half a bottle a day per man.

Each Sunday a full bottle was issued - half of it for shaving purposes. The only possible method of getting a swill was for six to join together, bore a hole in the sand, place an oil sheet over it and pour the six half bottles into the hole. The sixth man, of course, had a swill, but not a very clean one.

Then the battalion was to move to France. That night the camp was simply hilarious. Any change was welcome. Troops never looked far ahead and our worthy battalion was heartily sick of the blistering sun and choking sand of Egypt. Could it be true, however? It was. Before lights-out the orderly sergeant came round to find out who had no field service caps. Jack's was at the bottom of the Bay of Biscay, where it had blown from the top deck when he was acting as sentry one stormy night. All right, he would have to pay for another.

The next day the march back to the Canal began. It was windy again - a fitting farewell to a sandy country. The voyage back to France was very different from the outward journey from Gibraltar. A storm grew up the first night and the boat pitched and tossed merrily for three days. Jack did not mind. He had found his sea legs by now and, in any event, the storm had abated before that wonderful sail along the Riviera began. If only she could see that, thought Jack.

CHAPTER 2

The green fields of France made an instant appeal to Jack and his friends for they were heartily sick of the blazing sun and burning sands of Egypt. True, they were unfortunate in their first introduction to this new land, for as they were marched through the streets of Marseilles, sleet was falling fast and the mud soon soaked through their boots, rotted as they were by the sun and the salt water of the Suez Canal. It was a big change from heat so excessive that it had been dangerous to stand about even with sun helmets and neck protection and the men felt the cold intensely.

The journey from Marseilles was the most uncomfortable journey yet experienced, for the men were packed eight in each compartment of a corridor train. It was impossible to stack all the packs on the racks, so most of them had to go on the floor, with the rifles under the seats. The journey occupied 52 hours and, as there was no room for anyone to have a full stretch, nerves got very jagged and joints very stiff.

Despite these discomforts, men found real interest in watching the changing panorama of the French scenery and in airing their French on porters and passengers alike at the frequent stops.

At one station, rum and coffee were provided by the French authorities but generally the men poured out of the train and persuaded nearby engine drivers to let off steam into their billy-cans, so mashing the tea. Washes were obtained by swilling under station taps, in tanks or in any other available manner.

Occasionally a loaf of French bread would be bought from the station buffet, or a few biscuits or cakes but the money difficulty arose here and change was not too generous when English money was being offered.

The men were particularly struck by the prevalence of black in the garb of the women folk and the conclusion was formed, probably erroneously in many cases, that it signified mourning for war casualties.

At last the journey came to an end and there was some disappointment when the train drew up one noon at a junction, apparently far away from any habitation. The "Fall in" was quickly sounded, packs were shouldered and one of the most gruelling marches yet experienced began. It was not that it was a long march. Actually, it was only seven or eight miles but the men were in no condition for marching. Seven days on a troop ship, packed to its utmost limits, leaves little room for exercise. On top of that, the men of the battalion had spent 52 hours cramped in rail coaches where two consecutive hours of sleep had been impossible. The route was by a long, uninteresting lane, uphill most of the way and the men were utterly dispirited. Scarcely a word was breathed, except in complaint and the man who had dared to strike up a song would have been bitten.

It was dusk when a small village was reached and here the battalion had its first experience of billeting. NCO's told off parties into all kinds of farm buildings and sheds. There were no lights, which made matters worse, but there was, at any rate, a floor. How good it was to stretch one's legs. Very few even bothered to think of supper. Jack found himself with a dozen others in a tiny barn. It was good to lie down in the hay. In a very short time these dog-weary men were slumbering peacefully.

The next thing Jack knew, he was lying awake listening to the twittering of birds. He closed his eyes again. It must have been a dream but, no, he rubbed his eyes and gazed upwards through a gaping hole in the roof. And what was that? Was it really snow? Yes, in the darkness, the hole in the roof had not been discernible but there it was and about Jack's feet was a thick carpet of snow. Just then the top part of the stable door was pushed open with a clatter and the head and shoulders of a buxom peasant woman came into view. "Pas bon" she exclaimed, pointing to the hole in the roof. Here indeed was sympathy but it was helpless sympathy. The good lady of the estaminet across the road had no power to alter the rules and regulations of the British Army.

The morning was spent in a voyage of discovery about the village. It was quite an ordinary Picardy village, complete with it's tiny church.

That first afternoon, Jack had his first shock. He happened to stroll into the orchard behind the barn when he noticed half a dozen of his friends sitting about half-naked, with their shirts in their hands. What was wrong? "Oh, just looking for lice" he was informed. It was not two minutes before he had his own shirt off. No, he had none but, what was that under the seam in the armpit? He showed it to Ern. "Yes, that's a fat one, sure enough" chortled Ern. "Thought you had none".

Another cherished hope had gone up in smoke and, had Jack known that not for years was he to be permanently rid of these little pests, he would have been still more troubled. The hay that had been so welcome the night before had served Jack and his friends this scurvy trick. That night, a fresh billet was found for his party but the hay there was also a harbour for lice.

A week passed, in which the men passed through another course of musketry, while short marches gave them back their marching legs. Then, on Sunday morning, the march to the line began.

It was snowing again that morning. Companies were billeted all over the village and it chanced that Jack's company had fallen in a full hour before the battalion was ready to move off - a bad start for packs readily found old sores.

It was three days before the battalion eventually reached another small village which rumour had it, was only three miles from the Front Line trenches. During the third day's march, evidence had not been lacking that they were approaching the trenches. Back in their first billets in the quiet of night there had been a dull rumble which continued through the hours of inactivity while, at times, it seemed as if the very earth trembled.

On the third day's march, however, it was obvious from the noise that the guns were getting nearer. Occasionally, the men were halted and told to take cover in the hedges as an aeroplane zoomed overhead. Usually, it turned out that the aircraft bore the red-white-and-blue roundel which proved it British and no enemy planes took interest in the troops. The men were warned not to gaze up into the skies lest the white of their faces should be spotted. Wild rumours were spread of the havoc which had been wrought in such columns by attacks from aeroplanes or by long-distance shelling which they had directed.

At Bertrancourt, the present resting-place of the battalion, there was a pay-out of a hundred francs for every ten men. As this was given out in one note and the few shops and estaminets in the village had little change, very few of the men were able to buy anything.

It was from Bertrancourt that a small party of NCO's was sent up to learn trench duty. They returned on the fourth night and immediately became the centre of eager enquiries. "What is it like?" "Do many get killed?" "Are the

Germans always attacking?" - and numerous other questions but all centring round the thought that was at the back of every mind: "How shall I manage?"

Next morning, Jack was up with the larks - it was surprising the number of larks there seemed to be in this countryside - and took a stroll on the open side of the village. He could not help but be impressed with the beauty of the morning and the peace in the fields. Just then, not a gun crashed while the cattle lowed in the fields as if all was peace.

Always a nature lover, he halted by a bank, his eyes searching for the sweet violets he loved so much. Instead, he found a patch of Forget-me-nots. The sight brought home very near. "Forget me not, beloved" he whispered, as he placed one of the delicate flowers gently between the leaves of the tiny Testament he always carried in his breast pocket. That Testament opened automatically at a certain place from which a tiny photograph almost fluttered out.

Jack picked it out tenderly and gazed longingly at it. On it was a print of some gigantic city offices and on one window a cross had been inked. Jack knew that the cross meant that his beloved worked in that room. It was sufficient to bring sweet thoughts welling into his mind.

Had he known it, he was on the threshold of a new existence, for fast-moving events were to draw him into the vortex which was to cost England and the Empire at large, casualties which as yet had not been dreamed of. It was very fitting that, on this Spring morning, Jack, still free of the cloud which was to hang over him for so long, was able to spend a short time with sweet thoughts of an existence which seemed so far away. Comparatively speaking, he was still only a boy. In a very short time, a few months at most, he was to be turned prematurely old.

Had he but known it, preparations were already in hand for the greatest battle Britain had ever borne, and before that battle was over the fine battalions of England's picked men, the early volunteers, were to be dragged backwards and forwards through the mud and blood of stricken fields until their ranks were almost unrecognisable. Fortunately, no one, not even those in higher places, could foresee the events of the next few months, much less of the next few years.

But let us bring Jack back from his day-dreaming and back to billets. On his

18

return he found everyone in a fine state of excitement. At last the battalion was to move into the line. It was just the thing that the men had hankered after since September 1914. "This Way to Berlin" posters had glared down blatantly at these young men when they had offered themselves for the Army, and they had almost been promised that they would be in the field before Christmas.

But a second Christmas had found them in the Mediterranean. They had grumbled and sought transfers elsewhere, but all to no avail. Unkind friends had suggested that their battalion had been forgotten. If it had been possible, the long delay would have damped their ardour.

At last, however, they were to be tested against the German hordes. They were confident that they could hold their own, that they would win their spurs as others of the Kitchener army had done, but there is in every heart a doubt on the eve of a big trial. Shall I stand up all right under fire? (It is not fear, for the bravest of men have it). The only thing akin to fear about it is the fear lest the man shall be less brave than the others.

At dusk, packs were taken up and the trail to the trenches began - the trail that, like in the song, was to be a long, long trail, a trail that for some would only be short in this life before it led into the last long trail: a trail that for others was to extend backwards and forwards across the Somme battlefields, in and out of the Salient and across many other fields of battle. Fortunately, no one knew what was to come.

At the first shell, an over-cautious officer threw the platoon into artillery echelon. He was quite correct but longer usage would make him careless of such tactics. For the last mile before entering the communication trenches the way ran by a long avenue of trees. Here, even in the dusk, the evidence of war was plainly to be seen in the blasted trees. Occasionally, men stumbled into shell holes.

On the skyline, the gaunt ruins of a huge building showed up and, as it was approached, a silence came over the men for, lying in its shadows were still forms on stretchers - the Reaper's harvest of another day of the war. "All quiet on the Western Front" would read the bulletins but in each sector there would be stretchers like these, with their honoured burdens. "They are brought here to be buried just beneath the brow of the hill" came a whisper down the line.

The communication trench was entered in single file. At first, the going was not particularly bad for the trench was fairly good. It wound in and out as if reluctant to reach the front line. "Keep left for stretcher bearers" came the whisper and the moving men glanced down at a drawn, grey face. Another dozen yards and then another stretcher. Altogether, there were twelve. Those still forms and haggard faces were Jack's introduction to the realities of war.

Somehow, neither he nor his friends had ever realised that side quite in this way. They knew, of course, that warfare means casualties but no one thinks of casualties quite in that way. Even this respectful care for the dead seemed unreal for young men in particular think only of war injuries as those sustained in a magnificent charge. Jack and his friends were still to learn of the death one sat and waited for, the death that came like a bolt from the blue, sent by men who could not have seen the men they were killing, even if the ground had been even, for they were often too far away.

It was the men who could best stand this kind of warfare who were to win out in the end. It required a cool and lasting courage such as no other nation possessed to quite the same degree as those of British birth. They might not show up so well as their more dashing allies in the charge, but they would be still fighting stubbornly in 1917, when the more temperamental French were almost at the point of giving up.

As Jack and his friends progressed along the communication trench he noticed that occasionally it was quite easy to see over the walls. There were points where the cover had been blown away by shells and these shallow sections became more frequent as the front line was approached.

In quick succession, messages were now being passed down. "Don't talk, we are nearly in the front trench". It was like the approach of an army of ghosts except that absolute silence was impossible. A man paused for a second and the next man stumbled into him. Tin hats clinked against rifles. A man stumbled into a hole and there was a muffled curse. "Keep quiet" came back the whisper. "What does he say?" Wilf, who was almost deaf, seemed to bawl the question. "Hist" came an urgent whisper.

"Duck here for snipers" and the men crouched as they passed a gap in the trench wall. "This is suicide corner" came another hissed message, followed by "Mind the hole on the right" and "Beware loose duck-boards".

The warning was too late for one man. There was a splash which was calculated to wake a corps of Germans and he came out spluttering and cursing the Kaiser. Another turn and Jack found that they were passing men of another battalion. Some were standing on a raised part of the trench, which Jack realised must be part of the firestep, with bayonets fixed and their faces set towards the East.

"Is this the front line?" he whispered to another man in the bottom of the trench. "Aye, mate, this is it" came the reply. The man spoke in subdued but otherwise ordinary tones and, as everything seemed quiet, Jack wondered what all the fuss had been about. Perhaps it was a case of familiarity breeding contempt, he thought to himself as he staggered on. Staggered was the right word for, by this time, the relieving battalion were thoroughly fagged. It is one thing walking down a road; quite another stumbling along an uneven trench bottom in the dark.

At last, however, they were told to halt and soon the men whom they were relieving moved off. There were three men in addition to Jack in his firing bay and they decided that perhaps someone had better get up and do sentry duty. They agreed to relieve each other every two hours. Jack took the first turn. He peeped gingerly over the top for his first glimpse of no-man's land. At first he could see very little and everything seemed quiet. Gradually he could distinguish the dark posts of the British barbed wire. He had no idea how far the German trenches were away but, in the distance, when he strained his eyes still more, he fancied he could see similar posts about another sixty yards away. He decided that his job was to see that no one crossed the space between the two. It was a peculiar sensation to feel that the lives of others depended upon his alertness in spotting movement. It was very different from the experience on the Suez Canal where there was no reason to believe that there was any enemy within miles.

He now knew that the enemy was at least within half a mile for he had never heard of trenches in France being further than that apart. Moreover, he knew that the enemy here was at least as wary as he and that an advance would not be heralded by any clatter of accoutrements.

What was that? He fancied he sensed rather than saw a movement in the wire. For three minutes he stared at that point but decided it was a stationary post. The incident made him jumpy and, when a few moments later, something like a firework (in fact a Verey light, as he later learned) went up just on the left, he wondered whether he should alert his comrades. The thought that sentries all along the Front would have seen the light also made him pause. A few minutes later three similar lights went up and he was glad he had taken no action. Those lights fascinated him since they went up as if from nowhere and were suspended for a few seconds, lighting up a large area before going out, leaving the outlook more gloomy than ever. Jack thanked his lucky stars he was not out in no-man's land while those lights shone. He had yet to learn that, if a man stands motionless, even under a Verey light, it is difficult to distinguish him.

Yet another distraction away on the right - a solitary gun - banged away, soon to be followed by an incessant stream of others. He thought they were German guns but the shells seemed to be going well to his right. It seemed like a firework display as the heavens were lit up with the flashes until it seemed that they were alight.

The bombardment continued for some minutes and then died away as quickly as it began but Jack fancied he could now catch the splutter and rattle of machine guns. There was a sudden crack in front and he ducked involuntarily. He remembered dimly an instruction that a sentry should never take his eyes off the front. At the same time, he had learned that if a sentry kept his head perfectly still he was almost certain to pass un-noticed and would therefore be safe. Something hissed and whined past his head and there was another crack. That one seemed very near. This time he did not duck. An old soldier had once told him that a man never heard the shot that killed him.

Three times that night bullets whined by him and a fourth plopped into a hammock at the back of the trench. "That's hit the parados" he said to himself, feeling rather proud that he had remembered the official title of the back of the trench. The enemy sniper tired at this point and Jack was left in peace to finish his turn of duty.

A queer business, he speculated; not an officer has been round to see if we are here. The first time in the trenches and we posted our own sentries. Where is the sergeant, that little rat Tomkins? Jack did not expect he would be much use in the line. All right for "left-righting" in front of the Major but not much good if there is any risk about.

Had Jack known it, there was some excuse for the absence of officers. A platoon officer was not expected to be on permanent duty in the line. Jack knew nothing of officers' watches and he had no idea that NCO's took turns of duty. Still, there was good reason for complaint that no officer had yet been round visiting posts and the platoon NCO's were remiss at not seeing to the posting of sentries.

It would have been far better for the morale of the troops had the system of officering been explained before the trenches were taken over. As it was, Jack's estimation of officers lessened and events were not to bring it much higher for many months. He had always been taught to look upon an officer as a superman who would always be in the forefront when danger threatened.

How was the time? He peered closely at the gunmetal watch, the same one he had scanned on the Suez Canal: half past eleven, time to wake the relief. He roused the next man who grumbled sleepily but could not argue against the watch. A whispered conversation took place and he clambered on to the firestep with a warning about the sniper. Jack slipped down into the bottom of the trench, fixed his steel hat for a pillow, pulled his greatcoat closer about him and curled up for sleep. It was no feather bed but he was tired and sleep came soon.

CHAPTER 3

Jack's first morning in the trenches broke clear and bright: a typical Spring morning which brought larks over the trenches in great numbers. The first daylight glimpse of no-man's land was disappointing. Jack could not have told exactly what he did expect to see. That was the funny thing about the war; it simply knocked the bottom out of all preconceived notions. Everything was totally different from expectation.

What did Jack see by the limited aid of his periscope? Just over the parapet there were certainly a few shell-holes but nothing is less impressive than an old shell-hole unless it is an exceptionally big one. Again, the straggly barbed wire - not half so thick nor half so good protection as Jack had regarded as absolutely essential for the never-to-be-used trenches in the desert. Half the posts - it was a little early for the iron stakes of later issue - seemed so insecure that they might have swayed in a strong breeze, while the gooseberry and other formations with which he and Jim Foggitt had been so meticulously careful in Egypt were absent.

Beyond the wire, most of no-man's land was covered in long, coarse grass and weeds. The German wire seemed much more formidable and in a far better state of repair. Though Jack kept his eyes glued to the periscope for several minutes he could not see a sign of life in the German trenches. It was not likely that he would, of course, but he had not yet realised that it would probably be just as dangerous for the Germans to reveal themselves as it was for he and his friends.

Interest in no-man's land having subsided, Jack decided to view the trench. He passed along, exchanging greetings with his various friends and found that the trench was fairly good for the most part, though wide. He could not understand this until an old soldier of the Scottish regiment on the Right told him that it was due to the constant battering of shells and trench mortars.

This Scottish regiment took trench life very differently from his battalion. With them, there was no nervous whispering. Men bawled along the trenches as if they had not only a perfect right to be there but, moreover, as if the Germans didn't count at all. They were a tough lot and Jack learned with a certain amount of chagrin that their colonel himself led them on retaliatory raids if the Germans shelled them, a simple if costly method of preserving peace. He did not imagine his own colonel would follow suit. The Scots looked singularly fierce, with hairy legs below clay-marked kilts and Jack did not wonder that the Germans feared and respected the kilties.

Just then a stentorian voice yelled that breakfast was ready, which reminded Jack that he was hungry. There was no sign of food in his trench, though Ern reported that a party had gone out to fetch breakfast. In the meantime, Jack had to be content with an Army biscuit and a sip of water from his bottle. Though the sun was shining, there was little heat in it and the men were dispirited at their apparent neglect. Cold water was cold comfort. But the larks sang merrily on and, if only there had been a drink of hot tea, Jack felt that the world would have been worth living in.

Towards noon there was great excitement. The fatigue party had returned, lugging with them a huge food container in which was some warm stew.

Billy-cans were soon out but this providential meal was not to be enjoyed in comfort. Jack had taken only a few mouthfuls when there was an ear-splitting crash just in front of his firing bay. Dirt flew in all directions, no negligible amount finding its way into his billy-can. That tragedy was not at first noticed in the excitement, for men were turning to each other, the one question in all eyes being "What is it?"

It was a coal box - a clumsy projectile like a canister which was hurled from a trench mortar. It did little damage unless it fell in a trench. Old soldiers would have told Jack and his friends to watch for such, and how to escape them, for they came rolling through the air so slowly that they could be easily dodged. The next fell a little to the right but shorter. The war had begun.

For an hour, the trench mortar bombardment continued, doing very little damage. Then there was a new sound, bad enough but not anything like the canister bomb. No sooner had this explosion occurred than Jack heard a cry for stretcher bearers from the bay to his left. The rifle grenade had fallen on the edge of the parapet and the battalion had received its first casualty. Poor old Mac. He was the finest lad in the company. A gentle, clean-living lad, he had been placed in the roughest platoon. Jeered at, at first, he had won through until he was probably more respected than any other man in the battalion. To those rough lads in his platoon he was almost an idol.

Strangely enough, that was the last explosion of the day on this front but the company had paid its toll and Mac was to be the first to sleep beneath the brow of the hill.

The bombardment had had a strange effect on the lads. One and all had shouted and laughed to each other, while knees had knocked with excitement. It could not be called fear; it was excitement that made a man lose control of his nerves. But the death of Mac cast a gloom over the company and, indeed, over the whole battalion. It killed the idea of immunity. for the thinking man it left a question: "Why the best?"

"Why the best?" was a question which was to haunt thousands of men in the years to come, for it always seemed that the best fellows had to go eventually. They might escape today but what of tomorrow, and the other tomorrows?

That night, Jack and three others were told off for a new job - sap guard. Of course, none of them knew what the job was to be. It would have been beneath the dignity of any sergeant, or even corporal, to tell anyone beforehand what a job was to be. "You four follow me" was the order in the present case. "Bring all your kit in case you don't come back to this bay".

It was not a big job to collect kit. As the trench was naturally dirty, a wise man would obviously keep all his belongings in his valise, haversack or his pockets. The way led right to the end of the company's front, where Jack and his friends found themselves next to a hole in the front of the trench. "Down here" mumbled the sergeant, a he slithered, feet first, into the hole. Jack followed first and evoked a curse from the sergeant for putting his heavy boots on that worthy's neck.

When the sergeant slithered a little further out of harm's way, more progress was made. The party slipped down a steep incline for about twenty feet and came to a tunnel. The air was very hot and, as progress had to be made in a stooping position, perspiration was soon flowing freely. The sergeant, of course, carried no pack.

It was here that the Tommies found their steel hats of real service for in the semi-darkness - only the sergeant had a candle - they bumped the ceiling often. Finally they scrambled up another incline and found themselves in a small cave.

There were three men already in it and Jack's sergeant informed him and his friends that they were to relieve these men and a fourth who was on duty in a further cave, though a further hole covered by a blanket. Jack was detailed to relieve this sentry.

"Be careful when you move the blanket" said one of the soldiers, or you will draw fire". Jack slipped through and paused for a second in the darkness beyond. "Who's that?" said a quiet voice. "Relieving sentry" said Jack. Peering up he could just make out a shadowy form a few feet higher up some steps. "Come up" said the other "but keep quiet".

Jack followed the direction and found himself in what seemed to be a large but unusually deep shell-hole. "You have to keep a look-out all round here" said the sentry. "Here are some Mills bombs and don't be afraid to chuck them if you see anybody suspicious. They have captured this sap-head once and the tunnelers had a dickens of a job to get it back".

"What is this tunnel business, anyway?" asked Jack. "Don't you know?" replied the sentry. "This is a tunneler's sap. Underneath us run galleries to right below the German trenches. Eventually, they will take explosives to the end and blow the Germans up. That is if the German tunnelers don't get under us and blow us sky high first".

"Where are we?" was Jack's next question. "Well out in no-man's land. The greatest danger is from German patrols or raiding parties".

"They might pop over at any time" grunted Jack. "Yes" said the other. "The thing to do is to be ready for them. They don't like Mills bombs, I can tell you. Just two more things: don't come so high up as this in daylight and, if you do have to throw bombs, chuck them hard enough so that they don't fall back on to you".

Just then a German Verey light went up. It seemed very close, as indeed it was and it threw into relief all the shadows and projections in his new abode. "Thanks, Gerry, you have given me some idea of where I am, " said Jack, under his breath. He had taken it for granted that the Verey light was German, for he had never seen one sent up from the British lines.

Verey lights seemed as scarce as trench mortars and shells had seemed when the Germans were bombarding the company's trenches earlier in the day.

"A bit of a one-sided war", reflected Jack. "Our job seems to be to sit tight and be shot at. I wonder if the Bosch ever do show themselves so that we can use our rifles or if they ever do come close enough for us to fling a bomb." Jack was not to know that it was almost a court martial offence for a British battery to fire more than half a dozen shells a day. The Germans truly had the advantage then. As for trench mortars, there was hardly a handful in France worthy of the name. The deadly Stokes mortar, which was to prove so useful, was only just coming into use.

Nothing eventful occurred during Jack's tour of duty and he took a malignant pleasure in passing on the instructions and warning to his relief. The other brought him down to earth by asking if anything had happened. It seemed quiet enough and Jack was forced to admit that it was.

Back in the underground chamber he found a wire bed let into the wall and clambered in. He would have loved to pull his boots off and to loosen his puttees but this was not allowed. Soon he was fast asleep, for it was pleasantly warm in the dug-out.

At stand-to he was roused and he and two companions sat with fixed bayonets and bombs handy for eventualities. It was daylight when he took his next turn on duty and that the change was noticed, quietly as it was made, was signified by the soft thud of a bullet in the earth followed by the sharp crack of a rifle.

"That sniper's quite keen" remarked his friend. "Keep your head down, Jack". The warning was quite unnecessary. Jack had seen the earth spurt up and he judged the line of fire. The day passed uneventfully and the relief party arrived late that night. The sergeant came with it. "Had a good time, lads?" he queried. "Not bad" replied Jack and the return journey began. Sweating and stumbling they passed along until they reached the bottom of the incline towards the entrance. It was wet and slippery and matters were made worse by a party of tunnelers coming the other way. Jack was half-way up, labouring under the weight of his pack, when a voice yelled "Gas attack. Put your helmets on".

Gas attack or not, it was too much to expect a man who could hardly breathe to put on the sticky HE helmet and no-one took the slightest notice. It was good to be in the open air again although Jack was astounded at the scene in the trench. Every man was on the firing step, firing away like fury. Shells were bursting in all directions but no one seemed to be worried. The party hurried along the trench until they came to their own section.

"They've been bombarding us for the last half hour" said Jim Foggitt "and an attack seemed to be developing but I think we've beaten them off".

"What about the gas?" asked Jack. "False alarm" came the reply "it's only tear gas. Where are your goggles?" Jack realised that everyone except himself was wearing the motor-goggle-like contraption that was supposed to give protection against tear gas. Come to think of it, his eyes did smart. It was just as if he had pepper in them and there was a not unpleasant, sweet smell in the air.

His goggles gave some relief but there was enough of the irritating vapour in his eyes to cause real annoyance. Nothing seemed to bring real relief but closing the eyes was certainly an advantage. It was not really painful but irritating enough to annoy one.

Jack jumped on to the firing step, eager to have a shot but, whether or not there had been an attack, there was no German in sight now. Gradually the excitement died down and the men began to realise that it was raining. At first it was only a drizzle but it soon became a regular downpour.

At this stage of the war the men had Macintosh capes as well as leather jerkins, greatcoats and groundsheets. Even with all these aids to comfort, is there any place as comfortless as a trench in wet weather? Gradually, one's clothes become heavier and heavier with the weight of water. The cape springs leaks and sheds streams of water on the bottom of the overcoat which drags heavily. The groundsheet is called into use but the leaks still persist. Any movement of the head sends an icy stream down the neck and cold shivers run down the spine.

The floor of the trench becomes slimy, then sticky and finally a complete swamp. One sits on the firing step but that too is slimy and it is unsafe to lift one's feet out of the bottom of the trench. By this time, one is nicely coated with mud and wet and miserable. Nothing to do but wait for dawn and hope for the best.

It is an interminable night. The only consolation is that it is the same for the Germans. Or is it? Already there are rumours that the Germans have cosy dug-outs - even beds and braziers, and that only the sentries sit out in the trench. Meanwhile, the wet seems to have damped the ardour of the gunners, who are taking a well-earned rest.

Daylight gave little cheer to the desolate scene. The men were in a dreadful state, with mud all over them. Everyone had a three-day beard which made dirty faces look particularly grimy. Eyes also were red and smarting from tear gas and, where the goggles rubbed the skin of the forehead, many men has a rash which had been induced by the gas.

This day there was no hot food or drink, only cold fried bacon which, having been carried up in sandbags, was well coated with hairs. Still, it was food and food was necessary.

The day passed uneventfully until stand-to when there was an amusing incident. Shortly after four o'clock the rain ceased briefly and the moon shone through brightly. It was this that provoked the order which caused the amusement. Along the trench came the order "Fix bayonets and jump out on the parapet".

"A raid" thought Jack. He and his friends were just about to obey when an officer came tearing down the trench wildly explaining that the order, when it began, was "Keep your bayonets down beneath the parapet". Obviously the intention was to avoid attracting attention through the moon's rays glinting on the bayonets. No message was ever passed down a line of men without mistake. At midnight the company was relieved and straggled away along the communication trench to the support trenches.

CHAPTER 4

It was astonishing, how different one felt in support trenches. True, it was only a little more than 300 or 400 yards to the front trench, as the crow flies, a mere flea-bite for a shell and well within the range of machine guns. But it was the relief from the sense of responsibility of being the first line, Jack decided, that made the difference. It was no longer the responsibility of the sentries to spot the first signs of attack although some sentries had to be posted just the same and the trenches were manned just the same as at stand-to.

Indeed, there were many advantages in being in support this first morning. The disadvantages were to come later. One big advantage had been that Jack's party had found a bit of a shed where they had at last found shelter from the rain and where they had quite six hours of sleep. After stand-to another big surprise came in the shape of some warm cooked bacon and the first drink of tea for four days.

Then the letters came. There was tremendous excitement when the corporal came down the trench with a bundle of envelopes. Jack scanned his almost fearfully. Had she written? Yes, there it was, a neat, square little envelope addressed in the bold writing he had learned to love so much. He scanned every letter in order to miss nothing and then slipped off to a quiet corner to enjoy the contents. It was some minutes before he tore it open. There was something very sweet in the joy of anticipation.

"Many happy returns" it began and that was the first time Jack realised that this was his birthday. The trench faded away into the background and Jack found himself transported into a new world. Could it really be true that only a twenty-mile strip of sea separated his world of mud and suffering from the world in which she lived. Could it be true that there really was another world - a world in which things were going their normal round? It came as a shock to realise that, at Stagford, trams would be running. How long ago it seemed since one had seen a tram. A world where one could walk into a cafe, sit down, say a few words to a waitress and - hey presto - a meal would appear. It seemed unbelievable. Could it really be that, away over there - so near - people were going backwards and forwards to their businesses without fear of the consequences, heads erect and no danger of flying shells?

How little our own world is, though Jack, and how narrow our outlook. Yet these reflections sent bitter thoughts racing through his mind. Was it fair that the men who shirked should be enjoying that while he and his friends were undergoing so much? "You said you could do it" came the answer, in the words that had become the soldier's reply to any complaint.

"Many happy returns, do you remember your last birthday?" He did remember that beautifully sunny Sabbath morning. He had been on leave and she had consented to accompany him on a walk. To the joyous ringing of the church bells they had wandered along that lane so well-known to both of them. At the top, near the church, they had paused, entranced by the scene: the picturesque old vicarage, the matchless green of the village sward, the monument to the famous sculptor and the square tower of the old church, hiding itself diffidently behind swaying beech trees; the flagged path leading between worn gravestones and that famous old Yew that had smiled on William the Conqueror's men. Jack also remembered the confetti from a marriage the previous day.

As they stood, the villagers came along in stiff Sunday clothes. There was rugged old Farmer Haynes, one of the churchwardens; there were smarter people from the outskirts of the town who had joined the congregation of this church. Among them was Muggs, a big manufacturer who was also the other churchwarden. The local squire led his large family in through the wicket gate, bound for the high pew at the front of the church where their ancestors had sat for generations.

Behind the brave carriage of the squire is a hidden, yet proud sorrow. Only last week had been the news that his eldest son, who had gone out with his regiment in September 1914, had gone to join those of his ancestors who fell at Waterloo and in the Wars of the Roses.

The bells stopped and Jack and his beloved wandered away. These precious moments of leave were so priceless that not a single one could be wasted; especially that one sweet moment when he had claimed that promised birthday gift - their first kiss.

Every phrase of her letter was studied and every phrase brought with it sweet memories that would never be erased. Not that it was an effusive letter. In a sense, it was more the letter of a pal. Jack would not have thought half so much of his beloved if she had been too readily responsive to his ardour.

Rather it was the very fact that these tender moments had been so few that made them priceless. An effusion would have marred his dream, so noble and high an

32

ideal was he weaving about this maiden. Could she have but known how he was beginning to idealise her she would have been the first to point out that she was only human.

But to him at this time she was more than human. She was becoming a ministering angel, a buttress between him and the perils of the rough path he had to tread; an inspiration in time of trial and, perhaps greatest of all, the one enduring hope for the future. Always also these reflections were to prove a sweet antidote, an escape from the trying present

There may be those who, in times of peace, would regard him as a sentimental fool. To them I would say that they know nothing of the thoughts of these high-spirited young men who had answered the country's call. Since the beginning of the war, which had found them at a very impressionable stage, their lives had been saturated with sentiment . What were they? Mere boys who had torn themselves away from their ordinary existence in a cause which they believed to be right, for a country which they believed to be worth the sacrifice and to stand shoulder to shoulder with a handful of men who were hopelessly outnumbered.

Every one of them felt that he was fighting for his own home, for a mother, a wife or a sweetheart. It was this reflection that was to nerve them to leap out of the trench for the charge or bear the horror of the long bombardment. The war was too big a thing in itself - each was a mere pawn - but it was different when a man felt in his heart that he was fighting for all that was dear to him be it home, wife or sweetheart. It was just this that made the vast difference between the people at home and those in the trenches. The great majority of those at home never rose to the heights of those in the trenches. Yet the day was to come when the world would gloat over the weaknesses of these men - men made elemental by the brutality of war - while the excesses of munition profiteers were to be forgotten. Men who came home on leave returned disillusioned, embittered by what they had found - faithless wives, reckless waste on munitions and the like - yet they fought on, hoping on.

After breakfast, as there seemed nothing to be done for the time being, Jack and Jim Foggit wandered over the top to the ruins of what had apparently been a substantial farm in pre-war days. Although it was badly damaged by shellfire it proved to be still sufficiently intact to indicate that it had been inhabited by a fairly wealthy owner.

Instead of the usual refuse heap and cesspool in the centre of the square of buildings there was an ornamental pool in which Jack took a bath. It was not a long bath, however, for the explosion of a shell at too-close quarters sent him hurrying to an engineer's dug-out beneath the farmhouse.

There was a further surprise at lunchtime: hot stew. This time there were no interruptions. Two successive meals did a lot to improve the spirits and tempers of the men but hopes of a nap in the afternoon were soon dashed by an order to parade in the trenches. A busybody of a Brigadier General had walked down the trenches - the support trenches of course - and decided that they were in a shocking condition. He had even spotted matchsticks and cigarette ends. This unseemly litter had to be cleared away at once. By this time the men had experienced a good deal of the trying ways and moods of superior officers but it was felt that this really did put the tin hat on it.

"I expect he would like to see us fighting in patent leather shoes and bowler hats" and "He thinks it's a Sunday School party" and similar comments were hurled about the trench by furious scavengers. Nightfall brought more disillusionment. Even in support trenches, it seemed, nights were not for sleeping. Jack and his pals were warned off for a working party. They fell in at six o'clock and were marched along trenches they had never seen until they reached the entrance of a disused trench. Here, they were told that it had been decided to dig it out for future use. (The future use, though they did not know it, was as an assembly trench for an attack).

What a pity Tommy Atkins could not have been told more of these secrets. He would have put his back into his job and the secret would have been safer with him than with the red-tabbed popinjays who opened their traps so easily to dancing girls in towns behind the lines. The loss of the secret meant life itself to the Tommy. It meant nothing to these pampered mother's darlings who owed their red tabs to relatives in the War Office.

Even in the dark it was plain to see that the trench was almost overgrown with grass. It may have been five feet deep but the bottom half was filled with thick, slimy mud. It almost pulled off the gum boots the men had been told to wear for the job. The first task was to widen the top, for it was too narrow to work in.

The stench became awful when the mud was disturbed and it became evident that it was truly a dead man's trench. Jack had been told that there had been heavy fighting in this area in 1914. It was said that the Sucrerie at the top of the hill had been lost and re-taken from the Germans several times by the French.

As he hacked away at buried equipment Jack found himself trying to recreate those earlier scenes of conflict. Then he found himself hating those skeletons that had once been men. It was hard work and a big stretch had to be done before the men were allowed to knock off. A short rest was allowed and the officer in charge of the work came round with a canteen full of rum. Jack had no idea of the potency of rum but he wanted a drink of some kind so he took a swig and nearly choked. Then the fiery liquid sent a warm thrill through his body. He knew he would never become a rum addict but he realised that the potent stuff would be very useful when he was starved and drenched. Even then he would have preferred hot tea, but rum could be carried where hot tea was not available.

A halt was called after a further spell and the men trooped back along the trenches to their own dug-outs. Breakfast was served immediately after stand-to and the men were told they could rest.

It seemed only a few minutes - in reality it was three hours - before Jack was called to take his turn at sentry. It was raining again by this time and Jack found that he could scarcely see beyond the British front line.

It was surprising how many odd jobs could be found to do in support. Jack was detailed to fetch in dinner and he and another had to lug in a huge food container. These containers were easy to carry over open ground but in a trench they were the very dickens, catching on one's legs at every step.

Nightfall brought another job. The parapet of the communication trench near the front line needed strengthening. Once again, it was nearly stand-to when the party returned.

After nine days - four in the front trench and five in support - the relief came. The rain afforded them a cheerless welcome. By this time, Jack and his friends were thoroughly fagged, "done-in" as they put it. They stumbled and staggered over the duckboards as they made their way out of the trenches. The duckboards shot up at one end as a man trod on the other. The man behind either caught his shin or slipped into the mud with a terrific splash. But little mishaps like this no longer mattered. A man who has undergone so much gets desperate and one mishap merely becomes an incident in a long line of troubles.

Finally they stepped out on to the road. It was like stepping out of a grave. The four miles back to Bertrancourt seemed interminable and, when a halt was called for the company to close up, the men slumped into the wet ditch beside the road.

Jack must have fallen asleep. At any rate, he knew no more until he woke to find himself alone. At first, he was alarmed, for he had no idea where the company had gone, although he believed that Bertrancourt was the destination.

Just then, however, he heard the well-known voice of the sergeant major, who greeted him in a sympathetic manner, probably because he knew more of the trials of the past days better than his own men gave him credit for. "Come with me, sonny" he said, and Jack fell in alongside the CSM and his batman.

The new camping ground was a field covered in about a foot of sludge and, when Jack eventually found his section, the men were in a hut which was open at either end to the night winds. Naturally, the best places in the centre were taken and Jack found himself in the full force of the draughts. Still, there was hot tea to be drunk and he was soon asleep, despite his wet clothes.

Everyone had expected that the next day would be a rest day. Instead, the orderly sergeant came bawling round at 9am to announce that there would be a parade at 11am and clothes and rifles must be cleaned. Easier said than done. Greatcoats, trousers, puttees, boots and rifles were caked in mud.

That parade would have been funny if anyone had been in the humour for fun. But it was not funny for the men. The major had a liver that morning and few escaped his scathing tongue. Another parade was ordered for 3 0'clock and the cleaning process was resumed. By this time the men were sullen and as near to mutiny as ever they had been. Not unnaturally, they ridiculed this cleaning business. They felt that they were real soldiers now that they had actually manned trenches. Cleaned buttons and polished shoes were all right in England but surely there were more important matters out here. It was 4 o'clock before the parade was released and a rush was made for the nearest cafe. How good it was to sit there drinking coffee - made in the always-boiling pot on the weird French stove - crunching the sweet biscuits and smoking cigarettes.

After all, it was a good war. Moods soon changed. This was a life where the most had to be made of the present.

"Pas bon trenches" said the rather slovenly madame. "Pas bon, madame" came the reply. She had a brave heart, though. Her son was in the trenches at Verdun - at least he was when she had last heard. He might now be a casualty. She hoped he would be home on leave next week but who could tell? Only the good God knew. C'est La Guerre.

CHAPTER 5

The events of the next few weeks were to be overshadowed by later happenings. Nevertheless, they were important for they gave a foretaste of what was to come. They were also important to Jack as weeks in which he learned at first hand the type of warfare which had been in force since the beginning of the war. They consisted largely of periodical tours in the line, in support and in rest, with the rest period being the shortest. In between were periods which were outside these categories, when the battalion or parts of it were detailed as working parties. They then lived at Colincamps during the day. At night they were in the line, wiring, repairing broken trenches and carrying up stores and ammunition.

It was a time of losses which, though small compared with those to come, were still heavy in comparison with those suffered by divisions which had been in France a year longer. The reason for this was known to the higher command and was probably wrapped up in the reason for the division being brought to France though only gradually was it discovered by the men.

For the British Army was preparing for big things. Verdun was proving a heavy drain on the French. They were putting up a gallant and wonderful fight but the strain was almost breaking them. Heavy and consistent pressure was being brought upon British Higher Command to take some action which would relieve this strain. Memories were short in the war. It had been quite forgotten that Britain's part was supposed to be on the sea. The days when Kitchener was laughed at throughout Europe because he talked of forming a British Army of 50 divisions were forgotten.

The tiny expeditionary force of 1914 had been regarded as a mere gesture of goodwill but, despite its ruinous losses, it had been given more and more work. Where were the men to be found? First, reserves had been called up; then the best of the Territorial brigades. Battalions in India had been relieved by Territorials and formed into new divisions. Some, like the 29th, had gained immortal fame at Gallipoli. Other Territorial divisions had extended the khaki line in France. So too had the first contingents of Canadians, while Australian divisions had shown their prowess at Gallipoli.

This was not nearly sufficient. Gradually, the new army divisions of civilian soldiers, men from the office, counter and workshop had taken their places. Had Jack known it, these new divisions were pouring into France and the day would soon come when Haig had under his control in France a huge army; an army as yet untried, for the trench warfare of 1915 could not be described as a real trial.

There was an arduous time ahead for those officers of the Higher Command who pinned their faith in the new armies. No one doubted the zeal of these keen young men. The very fact of their prompt enlistment proved that. Their quick development in the training centres that had sprung up all over Britain had proved it. But the odds were enormous. The German Army was a magnificently efficient fighting force in 1914. It was easily the best, and the best-equipped in the world. Every man was a trained soldier and every officer was a trained officer. Moreover, the German command was highly efficient in handling large armies. The British Army was amateur from top to bottom, for its greatest generals had never commanded a hundred thousand men. In addition, Britain had never contemplated fighting the big conscript armies of Europe on land.

Furthermore, the German nation was organised for war. Vast munitions works, working flat out to supply an army of two or three million, was actually in being. When Jack's artillery announced a bombardment of the German trenches, it was over before the men knew it had begun. They were peppered by German shells on the afternoons of gas attacks. They replied with rifle bullets. British gunners were allowed about half a dozen shells a day. Trench mortars blew the British trenches to pieces but the Tommy looked in vain for a trench mortar to reply with. Casualties were excessive by comparison with those of the enemy.

True, these things were changing rapidly, but the change was to be hidden from the Germans and it was hidden as yet from Tommy. When Jack and his pals first saw a pair of 9.2-inch howitzers they thought that the war was as good as over.

It was a gigantic task to bring the British Army up to a pitch of strength and training to engage the Germans in a battle. Such offensive battles had been initiated by them up to now. Hence, Chappelle, Latutut and Loos were, by comparison, mere skirmishes. Something on an altogether bigger scale was necessary. It became obvious that the French alone would never strike the knock-out blow. That fact must have been obvious to all as far back as 1915.

Not only was it necessary to prepare the British Army; munitions works had to be made capable of supplying guns and ammunition to a standard which was as yet far below those of the French and Germans but which was an enormous advance on what had been achieved in 1915.

For the Big Offensive, plans had to be made on a scale which had been undreamed of at the War Office. Equally big preparations had to be made in the line. Assembly trenches had to be dug to house the attacking troops, saps finished and new ones dug. Barbed wire had to be provided. Our own wire had to be strengthened yet made so that it could be removed. Trench mortars had to be put in position, ammunition for them carried in, extra small arms ammunition had to be provided, new gas masks, more wire-cutters and more tools.

One of the many criticisms which was to be levelled at those responsible for the pending offensive was the lack of preparation for casualties. That was a just complaint. Extensive preparations were made but they proved at first to be inadequate.

Another vast task was to arrange for the victualling of the attacking forces and their transport up and down the front, as they moved backwards and forwards to the front and centre attack.

The scale on which the preparations had to be made was quite new to the British. Is not my title of amateur fully justified? It is terrible to think that scores of thousands of lives had to be sacrificed to pay the price of experience.

Jack knew nothing of all this. It was to dawn on him gradually as he toiled backwards and forwards into the trenches, loaded like a beast of burden and wearied to the point of collapse and revolt.

Each night at dusk, parties set off from Colincamps, sometimes armed with picks and shovels, sometimes with wiring tools, but always with the rifle and equipment without which no infantryman must ever enter the line and which was so galling an encumbrance when it clashed against a spade or pick.

Nightly, as they entered the trenches, they passed the line of still skeletons with their still forms. Others were writhing and moaning. Sometimes they would see a huddled form at the trench side, the steel helmet gashed like paper or with a finely-drilled hole through the centre. The toll was continuous and the working parties did not escape.

On one memorable occasion Jack and Jim Foggitt were with a score of others on a special wiring job. It progressed well at first, without any interruption from the enemy, though it was a fairly light night. Suddenly, without the slightest warning, there was the vicious rattle of a machine gun, followed by cry after cry. The gun had found its mark with the first burst. As one man, the party went to earth. Jack had never felt so huge at a time when he wanted to feel so small. But there was little less security on the ground than when standing, for the men were on rising ground which gave a clear field of fire to the enemy machine gunners. The man next to Jack gave an awful moan of agony as he fell. From the cries it seemed that almost everyone was hit. Thank God the machine gun had stopped. Whether it was just a chance burst that had found its mark, or not, no one could tell.

What of the injured? Jack and Jim Foggitt bent over the nearest. He was calling for his pal, a friend from home who had bolted for the trench. The wounded man was badly hit and in great pain. Jack learned afterwards that his stomach was cut to ribbons by four bullets that had caught him even as he threw himself to the ground. To make matters worse, he had fallen on to barbed wire and, in the dark, it was hard to extricate him and his equipment. Jack tore his hands badly but at last they got the man clear. They lowered him into the trench and stretcher-bearers soon bore him off. Jack heard afterwards that he died before reaching the dressing station.

Another man had been paralysed. A bullet had struck his skull and he was doomed to be helpless until, in far-away Edinburgh, a skilful surgeon was to remove the smashed bone, leaving him able to walk as well as ever but with a fist-sized hole in the top of his skull.

There were six casualties altogether, three killed and three wounded. No sooner had the remainder of the party taken shelter in the trench than Fritz began an intensive bombardment. When the guns lifted there was scarcely a sign of the barbed wire defences that had cost so much.

A keen officer decided that the work must continue and, grumbling viciously, the men began again. Remarkably, the rest of the night passed off peacefully.

On another occasion, Jack's party was wending its weary way to the line when they noticed that the line of stretchers was unusually long. The two companies in the line had had a bad time. Fritz had been raiding the line on their left and had put down a heavy box barrage that had cut off the two front companies. Casualties were 28 killed and 30 wounded.

Gone was poor old CSM Emmett, known to everyone in pre-war days as the commissionaire at a big city store. He and three others had been buried in a dug-out. Ernie Nott and some other had dug furiously but they had been unable to find any trace of them. Then there was brave Buster Smith who, though wounded, had kept on firing until he dropped dead. Every one of the casualties was known to Jack's party. But those who remained had covered themselves in glory. They had taken back the trenches left by south country troops on their left and the southerners had been able to re-occupy them.

Jack would never forget these working parties. Nor would he forget the return journeys when the larks welcomed them back to their warm tea at Colincamps. After sleep, the remainder of the day was spent in sauntering about the village in search of chocolate Prenier. Even that tasted good when no other sweet food was available. The hard-bitten woman who had refused to leave the village and whose cow drank from the rank cesspool in her ruined farmyard, did good business in chocolate. Jack never heard of what became of her and her cow when things warmed up and they were forced to leave.

One of the more desirable working parties was located at Colincamps, where a huge hole had to be excavated for a dug-out. There were vague rumours that it was to house a dressing station ready for the big attack. Still, it was a nice job when the weather was fine.

As the summer approached, NCO's were instructed to get the men used to no-man's land and parties would go crawling about in search of enemy patrols. Jack never had any adventures on these patrols. The Germans seemed content to rest in their strong trenches and dug-outs.

One day the company was detailed to dig an assembly trench just behind the front trench. They found the tape in the dark and began to hack away gingerly. It was surprising how many sparks seemed to fly that night. Every pickaxe found a stone and Jack's heart was in his mouth most of the time. It was not long before bullets began to arrive, which set the men hacking more furiously. The bullets mostly went wide but more than one glanced off Jack's pickaxe. It seemed an eternity before he was down a foot but this gave him a fine sense of security. Time passed until finally, most of his body was protected. A further two feet and the trench was done.

Next day, the Germans saw the newly-dug earth and raked it with gunfire. The trench was never used but, fortunately, it had cost nothing but sweat and frayed nerves.

By May, it was an open secret, that an attack was to take place at the end of June, probably the 29th. Then the battalion was drawn out to a village near Doullins to practise an attack. Shallow trenches had been dug in replica of the German trenches to be attacked. The men raided them repeatedly until every corner was known. This was done quite openly and, though the utmost secrecy was observed by the men, it was not unknown for enemy aircraft to fly over, while every villager seemed quite aware that something was in the wind.

Jack had many misgivings during these trial attacks. It was difficult, even out here, to get the men to take these mimic attacks seriously. Indeed, on one occasion the major was so upset that he completely lost his head and kept the men at it throughout their lunch hour. This did no good, as similar tactics had failed in England. Under such conditions, the work got consistently worse. It was no use shouting and cursing the men as they bunched at gaps in the imaginary wire. They simply refused to regard imitations as the real thing. The time would come when Jack would realise that, had such work been insisted upon more effectively – until it became second nature – many lives would have been saved. But, in a battalion like this, where almost every man was competent at least to be an NCO, it was very difficult to get discipline in the drudgery of repetitive work.

The training period was drawing to a close when Jack and some others were called out and informed that they were to become battalion bombers and that they were to pack up and go on a course. The first morning was occupied in settling down. In the afternoon an elementary discussion was held on Mills bombs. Rifle grenades were the subject for day two but, at noon, the men were suddenly recalled to their units and Jack was staggered to find that he was to be styled a battalion bomber, although the course should have lasted at least a week. So, even though he had never fired a rifle grenade, he became a battalion bomber and learned that he would go over the top, when the date arrived, laden with rifle grenades. Truly a strange war.

All thought of this was soon taken out of his mind by the announcement that the battalion was to move towards the line next morning. They did move, but not to the trenches. The new camp was in a large wood about six miles from the front trenches.

The wood proved a peaceful resting-place but there was still plenty of work to be done. Each day, the men were marched off in large parties to Colincamps. Here were enormous stores of materials: barbed wire, trench revetment material, trench mortars, trench mortar ammunition, Stokes mortars and ammunition, hand grenades and small arms ammunition.

The men were laden with these things and then had to begin the long trek to the line. It was a wearying game, for equipment and rifles had a peculiar habit of wrapping themselves about the reels of barbed wire they were carrying. Two journeys had to be made each day. One 60-pounder trench mortar box was regarded as a one-man load, or two boxes of three Stokes mortar bombs, or one box of SAA, two boxes of hand grenades or a bucket of rifle grenades.

This material was stacked along the trenches until the whole section had become a huge arsenal and Jack did not envy the troops who had to occupy the trenches during the preliminary bombardment.

Huge stocks were also placed in saps which had been dug out in no-man's land so that they would be easily available when this part of the line had been advanced. None of the men had seen such huge stocks of ammunition before and the only gleam of humour in the whole situation was the thought of the shock that awaited the Germans when everything was loosed off.

This work was carried on until about the 21st of June, when it was supposed to be completed and all was said to be ready. That night the men lay down in a state of expectancy for, on the morrow, the great bombardment was to begin.

CHAPTER 6

The preparatory bombardment for the Somme battle was, of course, the first really big bombardment put up by the British. As bombardments went in the war it was the first British effort that could be compared in any way with the bombardments put up by the French and Germans. Our own bombardments were only like large-scale firework displays. The first expeditionary force and, indeed, the later British Army up to this date had been woefully outclassed in this area.

Now, however, the British Army was to see the result of the big munitions push that had been waged in England. Though the results were small in comparison with later efforts, it was gigantic compared with anything that the British had previously done. The fact was that the British Artillery had been under strict orders to save ammunition for this effort – not only to accumulate reserves but also so that the possession of so much fire power should be kept as secret as possible.

Ammunition was now in such great store that, for a week before the infantry attack, the German trenches were to be subjected to so intense a bombardment that they should be almost untenable. We shall see later how successful we were in this effort.

At first, Jack and his friends lay awake at night in their woodland retreat listening to the thunderous roar of the guns, which literally shook the ground. Before they had turned in, they had seen the sky lit up with the incessant flashes miles away down below Albert. They used to wonder what was happening up in the lines.

One day, a patrol was chosen to crawl out at night into no-man's land to report on the state of the enemy's barbed wire. They went off: Jack's platoon officer, a sergeant, a corporal (brave little Cooper, killed later) and three men. While they were out, the bombardment was to cease for two hours to give them a chance – it seemed a poor one – of success. Exactly what that patrol went through no one knew. A shell killed one of the two men, blew the leg off another and wounded the corporal. It was said that the Germans held their fire – it was almost dawn – to allow the officer, sergeant and remaining man to drag in their wounded. They did reach the trenches by the time the bombardment began again. They were well down the trench when another shell killed the remaining man and splintered the wounded sergeant's leg.

All day the men awaited bulletins about that sergeant; a man of no education who had served in South Africa. He was a staunch fellow, absolutely dauntless. He had volunteered for that patrol but both he and the private who had lost a leg were on the long trail by nightfall. It was a sorry ending to a gallant exploit and it cast a gloom over the whole camp. Jack could not help feeling that it would have shown more tact to have chosen that patrol from a battalion that was not going to attack on the big day.

On the afternoon of the 29th a Communion service was announced. Quite fifty people of the battalion paraded for that service – a service always solemn but inexpressibly more so in these circumstances. How people in England would have been touched to see these gallant lads – so many of whom were taking their last communion – standing with bowed heads taking the wafers which were the field substitute for the bread, commending themselves to the keeping of the Everlasting Arms.

"Fight the good Fight" they sang and unconsciously thrust forward their chests in proud recollection of their determination to face whatever was to come, bravely as Christian young men. It was a service that would live long in the memories of those who came through.

As the men came away from the service they were met by others who proclaimed that the attack was postponed; it might not even take place as the Russians were supposed to have made a big advance.

Later that night, however, it was announced that the attack was only postponed for two days and would take place on the morning of 1st July. The same night, a field officer came round and addressed the men in cheery tones. He wished them God Speed. He was not afraid that the men from the north would be behind on the day of the attack. The testing time had arrived and he knew they would honour their native town and do justice to the long training they had received. They would be fighting alongside veterans who had already won their spurs but there was no doubt in his mind that they would come out on top. For every gun the Germans had on this front we had two, he added.

The huts were quiet that night. Thoughts were busy but it was not long before one of the platoon wits decided to liven matters up. Soon the men were rocking with laughter. Candle after candle spluttered out and at last Jack was left with his thoughts.

How sweet and yet how hard it was to think of the vision, so far away and yet so near. Sweet it was to think of those precious moments, bitter to think that they may never be repeated. He was not a coward. He had no selfish thoughts in that hour but he prayed that he might be spared for her.

Jack never spoke to the others of his vision, it was too precious for that. Some of the others were not so reticent. Joe Shaw would be thinking of his rosy-cheeked maiden. Tom Jones would be thinking of the pretty brunette he was so proud to describe. Cross would be turning his thoughts to a girl who wrote every post and from whom he received thirty letters in that delayed mail from Egypt. Would Sergeant Drill be dreaming of the vivacious little French woman he appeared to have made such a hit with back at Hebuterne?

Were they all hoping that they would be spared for their lover? There were one or two, he imagined, who, from their behaviour in the trenches would be most concerned about their own skins. He did not pretend to be a hero but he was not going to shirk this job now the real test had come. He wondered how some of those who had made such proud boasts in England, who had been so irked by the long delay, felt now. Probably they were no longer so martially inclined. He would warrant that that little runt of a sergeant who had been transferred to another company would not be left-righting it across no-man's land.

His thoughts turned to bigger things. How would the great citizen army fare as a whole? They had prided themselves on their physique, their aptitude, training and spirit. They had enlisted amid the blare of trumpets. They had had the glory. Could they do the work? They would win their spurs. When all was over and the dinted shield of Prussian militarism hurled to the dust, they would march triumphantly home, the pride of their town. His vision would be there, waving a tiny lace handkerchief.

Next morning there was a special breakfast – porridge as well as bacon. Jack remembered that condemned men were said to be well-fed and the circumstances seemed very similar.

By noon, the final preparations had been made and every man issued with the extra food and equipment he was to carry. They were to be prepared to hang on to their guns for at least two days. Each man had to carry two extra bandoliers of ammunition slung crosswise across his shoulders. He already had 120 rounds in his pouches and this made a total of 220 rounds. Each man also had to carry a Mills bomb in each of his side pockets. Feet had been rubbed in special oil to prevent damage when standing in waterlogged trenches. There were iron rations for two days: a bar of special chocolate and a sandwich that was supposed to be consumed just prior to the advance. Water bottles had been filled under supervision and were not to be touched under pain of severe penalties.

As a battalion bomber, Jack had to carry a canvas bucket filled with rifle grenades, a heavy as well as a highly dangerous load, for no-one had a very high opinion of British rifle grenades. This bucket was to be slung over the left shoulder. Each man was also to carry a pick or a shovel and Jack was unfortunate enough to be a pick man, a pick being the heavier of the two. This unwieldy tool was to be hung through the equipment, between the back and the haversack.

No one had great faith in the methods used to cut enemy wire – artillery and Bangalore torpedoes – so every other man had a wire clipper attached to the end of his rifle. Again, Jack was unlucky.

Trenching tool blades were to be slung across the lower part of the body as additional protection. Gas masks had been examined in the way that infantrymen did all such examinations. Field dressings had been explained, yet again.

In addition to the ordinary divisional coloured markings on the back of the shoulders, each man had to fix a triangular piece of tin on the back of his haversack so that he could be picked out easily by our aircraft so that they would know the progress of the division. Each of the four attacking waves was distinguished by coloured pieces of rag attached to the right shoulder. Jack's company was to wear brilliant red. The Major, an old Boer War soldier, tactfully remarked that he was giving no orders but a piece of rag might easily get rubbed in the mud.

Although all this equipment made a soldier look like a Christmas tree, there was a reason for everything. The two days rations were to ensure food where ration parties could not follow. The extra ammunition was to make sure sufficient was available independent of new supplies. The need for water was obvious. The picks and shovels were to turn the faces of captured trenches.

Nevertheless, Jack could not help feeling that it was overdone. It was all very well for a man to have all these things when he arrived at a captured trench but it was bound to impede his progress in getting there. That, it seemed to him, was the important point.

A couple of bombs might be useful to an attacker who had his hands free but they would be useless to a man loaded up as he was going to be. Indeed, he would have difficulty in getting them out of his pockets. It was no use pointing out the obvious flaws. These were just the ones that were never remedied in the army. Jack would not spoil his lunch over it.

The afternoon was free and Jack set about a task which he felt must be done before the morrow. He must write a note to his beloved – just in case.

It was not an easy note to write but, when it was finished, it was a brave note.

Grieve not. I have no fear for the future. I have chosen my course. Away back on 11th September 1914 I knew this day would come. If I could choose again – the easy course at home, or this – I should not hesitate. Those who would belittle the men who came say that many enlisted in drink. I do not know anyone who did. My choice was made not in a moment of excitement but after due consideration. I could see no other honourable course and I do not think you would have had it otherwise; even if then I had not meant anything to you.

I feel that I have taken a man's course and I mean to face everything that comes as a man should face it. No one could have foreseen this moment and all that it means. Heroism would be easy in defence of one's home in one's own land. It is not so easy when one is across the sea. It is not so easy when one is a mere unit in a huge force. Someone has to carry on and I can see no possible reason why another should take my place. If it is God's will that I should make the great sacrifice tomorrow, I do it willingly.

It is a great privilege that I do it for you, my vision, the vision, which has given me a fuller life than I had known or hoped to know. I cannot pray that you will forget me, dearest. At the same time, I pray that it may not be too hard and that sooner or later you may find happiness again.

It was a brave letter; a letter worthy of those high-spirited lads who had made their great choice with their eyes open. Their relatives and friends had no cause to be ashamed of them.

The letter was carefully folded and sealed in one of those flimsy grey envelopes, patterned inside, which were used so freely by the troops. When addressed, it was folded again and enclosed in another envelope marked 'Only to be opened in case of death'.

That note, written by a man of twenty-one, gives an insight into the minds of those young 'old' men. Many men of twice these years flinch at the thought of death. Yet, on that day, thousands of young men in the full promise of youth, facing their first battle, were thus facing up to the realities of life.

Jacked slipped the letter into the folder of his pay book. As he did so he saw the will form designed for soldiers. He smiled grimly has he thought that he had nothing to leave except his memory. He pushed the book back into his breast pocket and strode into the wood.

The birds sang, undisturbed by the rumble of guns. Life seemed unreal. Tomorrow, when thousands of men were being blown to pieces, birds here would still sing happily. Flowers would bloom, seed-time would move on to harvest and the whole of creation would move calmly ahead. At home, people would hear their alarm clocks and go to a comfortable breakfast. The working day would start and at night workers would seek rest. Surely there was something wrong; somewhere, at the heart of things, there had been a ghastly mistake. The Maker of all could never have intended this thing to be, for men to march steadily into the face of death, hurling their young strength at each other in an effort to blast life away. How futile it all seemed.

Jack turned for relief to his vision. In this poignant moment he thought of her as he had first met her. From beneath a large drooping hat two serious brown eyes looked into his as they were introduced. It was a lovely face, slightly tanned for she was fresh from the seaside. Normally she wore a fresh. healthy colour.

She was then just eighteen, above average height and with a graceful figure. She was an open-air girl, who had cycled since childhood. Her carriage was upright, her voice a rich contralto.

Jack knew that he had met his destiny. From that first meeting his small world revolved around his goddess. She was worth waiting for, worth fighting for.

The cookhouse call broke rudely into Jack's reverie. Tea proved to be another sumptuous repast and then there was another hour before Jack decided to don his equipment. He cast a hurried glance across the boards that had served for a bed and dashed out, complete with rifle, grenades, pick and other assorted equipment.

"Fall in here", roared his sergeant's voice. It was a parade just like any other except for the additional kit, although faces were a little more serious. Officers appeared. "Right dress. Form fours".

They were off, winding down the woodland track. Where this led into the roadway, hundreds of men of the sister battalion – a rough crowd of miners – had gathered. These rough men, who had at first looked with contempt on the milder-mannered men of the town battalion, now recognised that the others had proved their mettle and were ready to face the hardest task of a battalion.

It was a calm, beautiful June evening and, as the column marched through the village, their were signs that the locals had finished their daily work and were busying themselves about those jobs that all villagers have to do before returning to their lavender-scented sheets. Such scenes never failed to bring vividly into Jack's memory his happy boyhood days in a historic Midlands village. This was located many miles from the nearest town. In the shadow of its ancient tithe barn one might listen to the chimes of the village clock, the only sound to break the stillness of the night. The rustic scents such as new-mown hay, or burning wood, were like nectar to him.

Jack and his squad marched on. There was the old baker's cart; there was a young boy taking the cows to grass; by a cottage door, a woman was awaiting the return of her husband; there was a group of children playing an old game renewed by current events: soldiers.

Jack had wanted to be a farmer. He was a great lover of animals and he loved village life; especially the evening hour of rest from toil before early retirement. Long marches had impressed upon his mind the joys of food eaten with a healthy appetite and of rest when limbs demanded rest. He found himself enjoying the local scene, even though he and his comrades were moving towards the grimmest struggle of their young lives.

The men were determined to keep up their spirits. "There's a long, long trail a-winding" was struck up by someone and soon everyone was singing through the songs of wartime, even down to the threadbare Tipperary. The long, long trail was beginning in truth, but for how many?

The word was passed down that there must be no more singing. This brought home quite unnecessarily the seriousness of the situation. There was plenty of time for thought before morning. Jack stole a furtive glance at his comrades. Faces were set and stern and it did not take a student of psychology to know that thoughts were busy. He wondered how many had heard the call. Many a man knew when his time was drawing near.

Frequent halts because of the presence of other troops on the road made the march difficult and tiring. At Bertrancourt, the battalion did not take the usual road but embarked on a circuitous route for tactical purposes. How anyone expected to deceive the Germans by such an elementary move could not be imagined. Besides, did not every estaminet in the area know what was happening?

It was nearly 10pm – dusk – when a halt was called and the men were told that hot tea was to be served. The field kitchens were here, smoking furiously. The tea was welcome but there was little demand for the rum, of which there were liberal supplies. Rum drinking was regarded more as a joke than a serious necessity. The men preferred to face what was to come in cold blood rather than with muddled heads.

Nevertheless, it was not a funeral feast. Old Fats saw to that. Cap comforter stuck on at a jaunty angle, he pretended he had much more rum in his tea that he really had. He raised his Dixie lid high and toasted all the section one by one. He was a brave lad – a true Englishman – staunch and fearless, best shot in the company and a swimmer of no mean ability. But he would never be a real soldier. His ponderous bulk and easy outlook on life would always prevent him from drilling smartly or turning out spick and span in parade. One could not imagine him in a bayonet charge but there were other paths of usefulness in the Army. Not least was the role of the man who entertained his pals when conditions were bad, when rain was running down one's neck or when an ordeal had to be faced.

As a bandsman, Fats scarcely knew what trench life was like. The bandsmen had been withdrawn for practice until today they had returned to their companies for the attack. Fats, however, was not frightened at the prospect. He had never done a better hour's work than he did at that halt. Even the officers could not forbear to smile.

Glances sought the East. They were not looking for the sunrise today. They were gazing on the darkening skies as the sun sought its rest in the West and they were gazing nearer earth at the dark clouds of smoke from the belching guns and bursting shells.

Surely this next sunrise would bring hope - as do all sunrises - but what else?

Jack remembered very little of the rest of that night's march. They threaded their way through firing batteries and were almost deafened. They saw gunners stripped to the waist, feverishly feeding their weapons. They waded through trenches flooded by recent rains, dragging their heavy feet through sticky mud until Jack though he would drop from exhaustion. It was 4am before they slogged wearily into a support trench from which, three and a half hours later, they were to attack.

CHAPTER 7

By 4am the men had been on the move, apart from an hour for supper, since 7pm the previous night. Zero Hour was to be 7.30am. So used by now were the men to the roar of the guns and, indeed, they were so fagged, that they paid little attention to them. In any case, little could be done for on no account was there to be call for stretcher bearers. Jack supposed that the reason for this order was to avoid advertising casualties. It was an order which meant that ignorance was likely to lead to false rumours.

An order was passed down that each man should cut steps in the front of the trench so that he could climb out easily when the time came. Jack carried out the instructions and then slumped down at the bottom of the trench to rest. He was almost asleep when a figure loomed up. It was Ern. They shook hands and looked silently into each other's eyes. It was a wordless "God Speed". In this moment, each knew the other's thoughts as plainly as if they had been uttered aloud. For years they had stood side-by-side in a village choir. They knew each other's families intimately. That handshake also meant "Tell them I wasn't afraid". Ern was going to join his machine gun team. Machine gun men had about as much chance as bombers.

Such is the resilience of youth that Jack was fast asleep in two minutes. He awoke to a shout of "Get your equipment on". He staggered up and, as he buckled on his belt he noticed that the gunfire had risen to a crescendo, with a rhythmical regularity. He would learn afterwards that this was what was known as drawn fire. The heavy shells were pouring from the thousands of guns just like machine gun bullets. The rhythm was only broken by the burst of enemy shell all about the trench in which he stood.

Crump, crump came the 5.9's, throwing out dense clouds of black smoke. The earth throbbed and shook. To anyone in normal times it would have been terrifying. But a soldier who is going over the top is not normal, he is a machine with only one purpose, to go forward.

Whistles blew. "Come on" shouted officers and NCO's. The great attack was launched. For more than twenty miles men of a score of divisions were hurling themselves into the open. It was a time for hurling. It was a Herculean task to throw one's weight with all the necessary encumbrances up a steep trench wall. Men slipped back, cursing. Some fell noiselessly except for a queer gurgle or a sharp intake of breath. These were fated to go no further. They were the vanguard of a long procession for the long, long trail.

Enemy machine guns were traversing the trench top, but there were 200 yards to cover before the British front line trench was reached. In the open, Jack felt a strange nakedness. Never before had he felt his body so vulnerable. It was as if he had suddenly been stripped of all his defences. There seemed so much of him, yet with all his heart and soul he wanted to feel so small.

"Lie down a second until the line is formed" came a quick order. "Now forward". It began with a quick march that became a kind of amble half way between a march and a run. It would have been a run, only running was impossible with so many handicaps. The ground was all torn up and smoking. Ahead, there seemed to be nothing but smoke. There should be two waves of men ahead. Where were they?

A convulsive cry made Jack turn sharply to his left. Yes, poor old Mac had got it. His face drawn and grey, his hands clasped to his stomach, he staggered two more steps and fell. That momentary glance was sufficient. Jack knew that Mac would die. A strict order that no one should stop to help wounded men had been issued but Jack saw Sergeant Slim stoop as he ran and drag Mac into a shell-hole.

Mac, if he was conscious enough to know it, was safe from any more machine gun bullets. Jack reeled as a terrific explosion took place before him. A shower of dirt and stones rained on to his steel hat. Half choked with smoke, he found himself gazing into a yawning chasm. Fifty yards away, men might have been killed by fragments of that shell, but he was unhurt.

Swaying drunkenly, he lurched around the gaping hole. A flying stone from another burst caught him on the hand. Another thud close behind covered him again with dirt. He was still unhurt. Did he have a charmed life?

Bullets whistled and hissed about him. He bowed his head as if they were mere hail. Strange, what little things seemed to worry you at such times. He hoped he would not be blinded. A leg wound would not matter much, but he had a horror of stomach wounds.

Then there was that deadly bucket of rifle grenades that would persist in swinging round to the front. He was sure he would kick one into detonation or, worse still, a bullet might hit them and then it would be all up. How many times did he swing that bucket back? It was awkward, too, when he had his rifle, bayonet fixed, in both hands.

Shells burst endlessly. Jack's journey was endless. He marvelled that he had lived so far. To the right and left of him he was aware that men were falling. It could not be otherwise. A single man might live but the Germans would be totally inefficient of they could not hit someone in the row.

One man went head over heels. Another sank quietly down, a look of amazement on his face. He didn't seem to be hurt but bullets only make tiny holes where they go in. Twenty yards to the right a shell dropped right on the line. Six men simply disappeared. It must have been the same all along the line but the gaps filled up.

A shallow trench yawned ahead and Jack leapt over it. He was enveloped in the choking black smoke from another shell. This time he ran down into the shell hole, through the hot gases and up the other side.

He wouldn't do that again. He might get one in the face which otherwise would have hit him in the leg. Shells came faster, making him sway in his stride. Machine gun bullets multiplied. How on earth could anyone get through? The realisation came to him that he would not get through, that the whole attack was being ruthlessly destroyed. He knew then that he would never get through to the German trenches. That realisation seemed to solve a great problem since he had been wondering what he should do when he got there. Yet he kept on.

His breath came in great gasping sobs. It was not so much the distance he had come, nor the weight he carried, but rather the excitement. He could scarcely drag foot after foot.

A wider, deeper trench gaped ahead. It must be the British front line at last. It was so badly blown about that it was ten feet across so he could not jump it. He stumbled to the bottom and flung himself up the other side. Now he was in the real no-man's land. Ahead, he could just see a few odd khaki figures. What had happened to the two front lines?

Once more he glanced left and right. His own line was woefully thin but it was still advancing. The set, hard faces of his comrades bored into his mind. They looked almost jaundiced. Evidently the strain was telling and there was not a natural expression among them. He could not tell – he dared not look close enough to see – what was happening to his friends.

He was in the wire now. He wished he had not striven so hard to make it good. Fortunately, it had suffered severely in the bombardment. He picked his way carefully over it, strand by strand. It was useless to rush this part of the business. Bullets or no bullets it was no use getting caught up in the wire.

Even so, he was well up in his line when he emerged. Forward again they lurched on, then another terrific explosion but he was still going. Another close shell yet he was still unhurt. Then a third. He thought he was through at first but a sharp pain struck through his leg. It simply gave way and he fell. Dark blood was oozing through his puttees. He wondered if it were much. At first it would not move. Oh, well, it could not be helped, he would have to get out of it. Anyhow, what was the use of going on? There was hardly anyone left now; certainly not sufficient to do any good.

A corporal came panting up and went forward. His face was white and set. He was not only winded but frightened. He never came back. Jack staggered to his feet. At first he swayed drunkenly but it never occurred to him to crawl. Dragging his wounded leg behind him he limped painfully back to the trench. It did not seem to matter about the bullets now.

Carefully, he again picked his way over the barbed wire. He was almost through when a sudden excitement seized him. Whether it was the idea of the comparative safety of the trench ahead, he never knew but he was suddenly possessed with a wild desire to get out faster. He tore at the wire but the more frantically he tore the slower became his progress. A close bullet, which pinged on the wire, brought him back to his senses and made him realise that he was giving the snipers a better chance. He calmed down and was soon free to stagger, exhausted, into a bay of the front trench.

He almost fell on top of Darkie Moon, who had caught one on the back of the leg. Then, with a tremendous clatter, Waggie Watson also fell in. He was hit in the shoulder. None of the wounds was really serious and they bandaged each other up. It was a rough and ready job, for hands were none too steady and shell were bursting all about.

Their position was obviously untenable for long and the initial sense of relief at finding themselves safe from machine gun bullets soon gave way to concern as shell after shell burst dangerously near.

Where were they? At this point, the ground fell away slightly for a short distance before rising to the support trench from which they had attacked. Darkie thrust his head round the traverse to get a wider view of the land. He withdrew, blood streaming down his cheek. A sniper's bullet from the flank had gone in at his open mouth and out through his cheek, leaving a neat puncture wound but missing his jaw entirely.

The presence of a sniper seemed to be blocking their only way out. Eventually, Waggie and Darkie decided to take the right turn of the trench but Jack chose the left. He was going by instinct, for the others, as scouts, knew the trenches better. That was the last Jack saw of the other two for many months. It was the last they expected to see of him, they afterwards related, for they were convinced that he had made the wrong decision.

Jack crawled to the left, dragging his injured leg behind him. In the next bay, he found four dead men lying in different positions, hugging their rifles. Two were half buried, one was almost sitting up and a fourth lay as if asleep but the pallor of his face told its own story. Jack raised himself to crawl over the bodies. Immediately there was rip-rip of bullets and he felt one tear through his haversack. This would not do, he thought. The sun reflecting from the tin triangle on his haversack must be attracting the sniper's attention. He dumped his equipment, except for his rifle and the bucket of grenades, and pressed on.

In the next bay there were three dead men but a fourth was moaning piteously. At sight of Jack he pleaded to be bandaged. His legs were broken but he only seemed worried about a great head wound. It seemed to Jack that one side of his head was blown away. Blood dripped from the raw flesh. Where there should have been an ear was only a tiny hole. It was a case for a shell dressing but he pleaded so hard that Jack took out his field dressing and tenderly tied it about his head. It was a poor job but it sufficed to soothe him and he sank back with a hoarse "Thanks,matie". Jack felt only a fierce resentment against the enemy gunners who, having destroyed that attack, were now tormenting the brave men who were dying.

He lost count of the dead and dying men he saw that morning. His mind was numbed by the horrors he experienced and he keenly felt his own helplessness. Where were the stretcher bearers? They had been told to advance only when the German trenches were taken. What foolishness!

Heavy shells were pounding the parapet. More than once the force of a near explosion lifted Jack's steel helmet but he still escaped further injury.

"It's hell here", pleaded more than one badly wounded man. "Can't you send the stretcher bearers to get us away?" How long these poor fellows had been lying here, Jack could only surmise, for most of the men in the trench belonged to the brigade which had been holding the trench for the bombardment.

A pioneer sergeant dashed along the trench. He was the only man whole. He had gone over with sixty men, he said, and he was the only survivor. What was he to do? It was easy to tell him to report to an officer but where would he find one? Jack was certainly not going to advise him to take to no-man's land again. What use was one man where sixty were required? What was the use of it all anyway? Someone had made a sorry hash of things.

By now Jack was beginning to realise that he was lost. He caught sight of some man at the entrance to a dug-out. "No room here" they bawled, before he had time to speak. "This place is full of wounded". "No one wants to come in", replied Jack. "You'd be better to get out yourselves. Where is the communication trench?"

"Right in front" came the reply and Jack realised that the trench lay before him. He had missed it because the end was blown in.

"Mind the snipers", someone warned him but he had to get over the heap of dirt at the opening of the trench. Oh, well, it was all in a day's work, he thought and over he went. It was wonderful to see three yards of good trench ahead and he pushed on. For the most part, trenches merged into a pock-marked wilderness of shell holes. Fifty yards on, he met a stretcher bearer he knew. As he bandaged Jack's leg, he asked what was happening in the line.

Jack's story appalled him but he went bravely forward and Jack learned later that he had done wonderful work. He lived through the war, too. His last words to Jack were "Don't stop at the Basin, push on". The Basin was the most advanced dressing station. It was in reality a basin that had once been a wood. All that remained now were three splintered stumps.

At the Basin Jack found a shocking state of affairs. The dug-outs under the lip were being used by the medical men but, lying out in the open, were hundreds of more-or-less severely wounded men, awaiting what attention was possible. Never had Jack seen such a sight and he could not help thinking that the men would have been better off where they had fallen, for a single well-placed shell would kill scores here.

Jack was very glad to be ordered on. "Get as far as you can, sonny, " urged a kindly sergeant, but Jack first told him the state of affairs in the front line. It was a wearisome business, this trench crawl. For hours, it seemed to Jack, he dragged himself on, eyes fixed on the gaping hole in the heel of the man in front.

With a feeling of relief he came to a machine gun post of the Durhams. At any rate, someone was in a fit condition to hold up any counter attacks. These men were hammering away for all they were worth with a Vickers machine gun but one of them paused to give Jack a drink.

Jack crawled onwards, around a ruined farm building. He did not know, but he was close to a trench in which one of his home pals had been killed by a shell. Only just out of hospital, he had been carrying rations when a shell killed the whole party.

Exactly seven and a half hours after the attack began, Jack emerged from the communications trench on to a road. Here he found an extraordinary state of affairs. Although the road was in full view of the German trenches, the field guns were out in the open. Stripped to the waist, the gunners were ramming shells home as fast as human hands could move. Two limbers galloped up, horses sweating, men cursing. The drivers jumped down and the shells were thrown off as if they had been harmless toys. The artillery, at any rate, were doing their bit.

Ambulances, including even the old-fashioned horse-drawn types, were driving right up to this section. "Winning, aren't we" said one of the drivers. Is there anything left to be winning? Thought Jack, but kept this to himself. He would not disillusion these men who were working so enthusiastically. Just then an officer approached. He was helping the wounded. "Do you think you can walk?" he asked. "If you can get to Colincamps it will relieve the ambulances for the stretcher cases."

"I'll do my best" replied Jack. "Then walk with this man" said the officer. "He's only shell shocked."

Shell shocked he was, if any man was. There was a wild glare in his eyes. His hands were trembling wildly. A shell screamed over and down he went, as if to burrow under a pebble. "Come on, lad" said Jack "It's miles away." He quite forgot his own troubles during that last mile for this lad was in such a state that he was down on his face every few minutes. It was impossible to calm him and remonstrance was futile. He was frantic with fear.

Colincamps was like the Basin all over again but worse. For half a mile along the road, stretchers were laid end to end. On each was a man. Sometimes it was hard to recognise him as such. Jack's platoon officer was one. Another was the officer who had commanded the platoon earlier. Both had taken machine gun bullets in the legs. Both were good officers but the younger had sometimes been priggish. In the line, however, he had made good. Now they greeted Jack as an equal. Wounds removed barriers of rank in this place, whether or not they were restored in hospital.

A sergeant who had been reduced for some petty crime was coughing up thick blood, his face ghastly. Jack sought news of his comrades but could learn nothing. Almost every officer was killed or wounded.

A Medical Corps sergeant too a look at Jack's leg. He wrote out a card and pinned it to Jack's tunic. 'GSW left leg' it read. "Have you been inoculated?" he asked. "Twice for typhoid and twice for cholera" was the reply. "Not for tetanus today? Open your tunic".

Jack was stabbed with a needle and his pay book was marked before he was pushed into an ambulance. It was dusk when he alighted at a forward collecting station. An orderly brought him a Dixie of soup and he realised that he had not eaten since 4.30am. Sleep was impossible. It was not that the plank bed was hard but who could sleep among those groaning men? Every now and then orderlies carried them out to die.

A general came to visit. "Never mind, boys he said. "You've finished with the war now. It will all be over by the time you are fit again. We have given the Hun something to think about this time, or rather you have".

Jack wondered whether he knew how things had gone, or was the general thinking of a place where things had gone better.

Next day, after another ambulance ride, Jack found himself at a CCS (casualty clearing station) close to the village where his battalion had trained for the push. What an eternity had passed since those optimistic days!

CHAPTER 8

The tragedy of 1st July 1916 burst with stunning force on a Britain not as yet trained to receive such heavy blows. Those dreaded brief messages were received in thousands of homes – in the manor and in the cottage, in suburban houses and in the long rows of artisan dwellings. Neither were the courts and alley spared, nor rural village, hamlet or great house. Others were worried because they had heard nothing.

Women wiped away stealthy tears. Their sorrow would not go away. That was his favourite chair. On the bookcase were the last books he had been reading. His hat and coat hung in the hall.

Gradually, as the same tale was told everywhere, Britain began to realise how costly had been the victory, for victory it was, though the reward was small. Not for years would people learn how great a victory had been won. Not for years would they realise that British youth had passed successfully through a test that seemed impossible to the military mind.

Never before had untrained levies been called upon to take the field against a superbly trained army. Yet these spirited lads of Britain, who had forsaken the ploughshare for the sword, who had left loom and factory, office and classroom had, at the call of their country faced enormous odds, and won through.

Backed by an altogether inadequate artillery, worked by men as amateur as themselves, directed by staff officers who had never looked to control army corps, they had attacked the finest army in the world, in the strongest entrenchments ever dreamed of and had shaken not only the line but also the superb confidence of a hitherto-invincible army. These facts were not yet realised but the tragedy remained.

Hitherto, Britain had had no experience of the enormous casualties attendant on such immense operations. Mons, Lors, Neuve Chappelle were local attacks compared with this sweeping move. Even Verdun was to pale before the immensity of this great battle.

In Jack's home town every street was in mourning. Thousands of people recalled that sunny morning when a fine battalion had marched out to camp, confidently expecting the day when having won its spurs, it would march back triumphantly. The laurels were won but there would be no triumphant march.

Jack knew nothing of this when, on Sunday 2nd July, he took the next step of his journey to hospital. He found the Casualty Clearing Station in a huge field by the railway line. Ironically, it was within a stone's throw of the fields on which he and his friends had charged so many times in preparation for the great day. There were about 20 large marquees in the field. In some of them, doctors and nurses were working frantically; for how long, he had no idea.

The field was crowded with men, many on stretchers but with many standing about nursing bandaged arms or legs. There was a huge queue for each marquee where the doctors were at work and he was told to get into one of them. It was well towards mid-day when his turn came.

The doctor cut open his trouser leg and probed the wound until he found a piece of shrapnel. "Got it" he said. "It will soon be better though it might be stiff for a few weeks. The muscle is lacerated but it has just missed the bone." Iodine was dabbed on the wound and an orderly told Jack to rest in one of the marquees.

He was hungry but there was little chance of food with this army of men. Jack found a pal in one of the marquees. He had been hit in the arm. Suddenly there was a rush to the outside. Jack and his pal went to see what the excitement was about. An indescribable sight met their eyes. An ambulance train had drawn up and was besieged by wounded men, with those on stretchers pleading to be helped.

An officer appeared. "Steady, men, there will be plenty more trains" he said. He might as well have talked to the incoming tide. Somehow, the idea was abroad that the men on the earliest trains stood the best chance of getting to Blighty and they pressed towards the train in dangerous excitement. A few helped the stretcher cases but, for the most part it was every man for himself.

When the train was full the men fell back. With every train the scene was repeated: the mad rush, the moans of the most severely hurt and the official appeals for steadiness. Another thing that upset the men was that there seemed no prospect of food.
A red-tabbed senior officer was summoned. He appealed and he threatened

but his threats were simply jeered at. These men had been through so much that there was nothing here, away from the shells, that they feared.

"Go home. Go back to Boulogne" they yelled and, of course, there were so many of then that no one could be picked out to blame. Finally, a battalion of Highlanders was requisitioned and one had the spectacle of a battalion of soldiers, bayonets fixed, guarding a crowd of casualties.

Jack was later told that ten thousand men passed through the Casualty Clearing Station that day. It was dusk and he was thoroughly fagged when he found a place on an ambulance train. On the bed next to him, a badly injured man was raving and asking for his mother. The ambulance train attendants worked over him and over all the serious cases through every minute of the journey. A drink of hot tea soothed Jack and he was soon dozing but his fitful dreams were disturbed by the groans and cries of his neighbour. The train slid slowly and smoothly along and Boulogne was reached at daylight. Motor ambulances conveyed the men to hospital.

Preparing to take a bath, Jack realised that he had not taken his boots off for three days. On the way to the trenches he had passed through a lot of water. Since then it had been very hot. His boots were simply baked to his feet and he had to call for assistance to remove them. His socks were in an even worse condition and there was scarcely an inch of skin on his feet when at last they came off.

Soon, however, he was happily in bed. Never would he forget that hospital. For days he lay there in snowy sheets enjoying the cool efficiency of it all. It seemed years rather than many months since he had seen a white sheet. After the mud and filth of the line it seemed like Heaven on Earth.

He loved to watch the Sister in charge. She was a tall, severe-looking Scotswoman but she had a kindly smile for everyone. She wore South African decorations and that alone gave the men confidence. The most serious cases became calm in her presence.

Yet there was something that prevented the men from settling. A short 21 miles away over the waves lay home. "You boys have seen the last of this war", an officer had said but, as the days passed, the men realised that this was not so. Meanwhile, Jack had time to piece together the tragedy that had overtaken not only his battalion but many more.

It was here that names like Gommecourt Ward, Beaumont Hamel, Thiepval, Fricourt and Mamety began to have new significance. Jack met men from all of them and all told the same tale – long lists of casualties. From the less seriously wounded of his own battalion he learned of the great – and futile – losses of his own pals.

Jim Foggitt, game to the last, had been shot through the head when sniping from a shell hole. Ern, his chest torn apart, had smiled bravely as he was lifted into the ambulance but died in the ambulance train. Jack Brat, on ration party, had been blown to pieces. Poor, brave old Fats, always clumsy, had been caught by a sniper when moving between shell holes. He had fallen in, dead.

The corporal who received and wrote so many letters had never been seen again. Sergeant Slim, who had dragged the wounded Mac into a shell hole, was blown to pieces. Still, the great bomber, was dead. Straw, the famous musician, had staggered, dying, into a shell hole.

Only two officers had escaped uninjured. Major Hoette, (D Company), Captain Moore and Captain Clark, (A Company) were dead. Clark was never fitted for soldiering but was the gamest of them all. He had died leading his men on.

Lieutenant Storry, the swimmer who had won all before him in Suez, had his legs smashed. Lieutenant Carr, the young graduate and the finest runner in the town was gone. Lieutenant Eldon, the doctor's son, was simply lost. His body was found twelve years later.

When the roll call was held, only 23 unwounded men could be found. Over 650 had taken part in the gallant charge.

As he lay in hospital, Jack pictured that tragic roll call. Where were the 23? Was Tom one of them? Had Reg got through? What a pathetic sight it would be, the ruins of a splendid battalion. They had been so full of promise.

He recalled the day he had enlisted with Pat Matlock. Pat had died of appendicitis in the desert. At least he had escaped this. There were a dozen others – youths he had met at business, youths he had walked with on nights off duty. Five of them besides Pat were only sons. Fats had no mother but, to his father, he had been a real pal. What hopes Ern's father and mother had centred on him. They had been determined to give him every chance. Then there was that fierce old man, the father of Jim Foggitt. Only the previous Christmas he had lost his other son. It seemed to Jack that the bottom had fallen out of everything.

The future life of their town would suffer too. There were men of great promise in the battalion – scholars, doctors, journalists, musicians, teachers, engineers and business men. It had often been said that they should never have been allowed to join one battalion. They had talents which might, with advantage, been split up in an army corps. But they would not have it. They had enlisted as pals and they meant to be pals.

Safe jobs were refused with scorn. Jack himself had been offered and refused a job which would have ensured his safety. Like all the others he wanted a rifle and bayonet. The appeal to be a man had gone right home with these men. They laughed with scorn at the thought of immunity from dangers that others were to face. If anyone can do it, I can, was the motto of every man. The phrase "You said you could do it" was the reply to every grouse.

The long months of training had proved irksome to their proud spirits. Why were others allowed to go when they were still forming fours at home? In their hearts they were just a little ashamed of the trip to Egypt, so fearful were they that it would be thought they were being pampered – given special care because they were their fathers' sons. True, many of the rankers were brothers of some of the officers. Many, both rankers and officers, had been born in the best homes in the town. They asked no favours on this account and were fearful lest parents or friends should be demanding it for them. They had trained together as pals. When circumstances allowed, officers. NCO's and men chatted together as pals and now they had bled together as pals.

Now that it was too late, Jack realised what a shocking waste it had been; not that he had any foolish ideas of his own importance. He knew that he could easily be replaced at home but there were many others who had shown signs of the genius that was within them

Now they lay side-by-side on that battlefield. He could visualise now what his stunned mind had been incapable of seeing during the charge. He could see the khaki-clad figures falling. He could see the haggard faces and the contorted forms. Mangled steel helmets littered the ground. Smashed rifles lay everywhere, with bomb fragments and shell cases. He thought with a shudder that men who dig trenches there in the future would curse as he and his friends had cursed when they had dug trenches and encountered skeletons and equipment.

These men who had hoped so much, who had determined to carry the good name of their town with honour and to write pages in its history, were gone. More than 300 of the 650 who charged would be buried near where they fell. The survivors would be scattered among other battalions.

Their attack had failed. It was too early for him to appreciate that it had failed gloriously. He could not yet see that defeat might be as glorious as success. Jack, that great journalist who had aimed to make an epic of the way the lads had gone forward dauntlessly – and as uselessly as the Light Brigade, had not yet taken up his pen. To Jack, there had been no glory in those steadily advancing waves, decimated by murderous fire. He did not yet realise that the battalion had done all that could be expected of it. He sought to excuse the failure.

His despondency was not lightened by the tales of others. Shy lads from the Home Counties, perky Cockneys, raw-boned lads from Scotland – all told the same tales of heavy casualties and none could see any advantage gained.

As he considered matters, he came to believe that nothing more could have been done and the fault must have lain elsewhere. Something would have to be done if the same tale was not to be repeated again and again until the British Army was finished.

He knew nothing then of the splendid German dug-outs, otherwise he might have grasped one reason why success had eluded their eager grasp. He did realise that it was something to do with the artillery. The bombardment had been terrific. It was said that nothing could live in it. Yet everyone told the same story of a full German line from which men shot down the advancing waves with impunity. Why was this? In those days, the creeping barrage, later perfected by the British, was unknown. The real problem was that the British artillery had lifted from the German front line trenches too soon. German soldiers, safely hidden in deep dug-outs, had emerged as soon as the guns lifted and poured a devastating fire on to the oncoming troops. Human flesh could not withstand the fire. All the theories that had been so carefully drilled into the men had been exploded.

Everyone agreed that officers, Lewis gunners and bombers had all been picked off first. It was all very well to send over Pioneers to consolidate the captured trenches but the trenches had to be captured first and the men got over. It was all very well to carry picks and extra ammunition but surely the first essential was to get over quickly and subdue the enemy. The Australians soon decided this for themselves.

The two miners' battalions that should have supported the attack of Jack's battalion had lost almost equally with theirs. Their advance should have been completed had Jack's battalion been successful but, as things went, a dozen battalions might have attacked in succession with the same result.

Men from all parts of the line told the same story. Withering machine gun fire had simply destroyed their ranks. They had no chance. The German troops seemed unhurt and were able to do all they desired. Horrible stories were told of callous snipers who had poured shot after shot into the wounded for the pleasure of seeing dying men squirm. Jack came nearer to real hatred of Germans than at any part of the war.

So far as he could tell, the advance had failed almost everywhere. He became convinced that present tactics would never succeed. Night after night he thought over these problems but there appeared to be no solution.

In the convalescent camp Jack met an old friend. He sat down to breakfast one morning beside an Australian soldier. "I know you" said Jack. "And I know you" said the Australian. They had been at school together and Jack did not know that the other had gone to Australia.

During the days he remained convalescent Jack had reason to bless that meeting for, although the canteen was full of good things – things he had not tasted for months – he had no money. Apart from his wound, which still troubled him at night, he was quite fit and it was galling to one with his healthy appetite to see before him good things which he could not buy. Fortunately, the Aussies were well supplied with cash and his old friend was generous.

Jack was glad that he had only to spend two days at Elverdinghe. This base camp was a thing of horror to men who were down from the line. Staffed partly by old men who should have been in glass cases, at home and partly by others whose chief occupation in life was to keep their jobs lest perchance they might be called upon to face the enemy, it was a place to be shunned like the plague.

The very atmosphere of the place was repulsive. It seemed to bring out all that was worse in the men who wished to shirk. Parades were dodged lest they might be parades to choose drafts. Decent men longed to shake the plentiful dust of Elverdinghe off their feet.

Jack saw some shocking cases of unfair treatment. Apparently those in charge were continually harassed by appeals for drafts for the front line and it rapidly became known that men who had no bandages showing must go. Jack remembered one man of 51 who was unable, through a wound, to close the trigger finger of his right hand, being sent to the front line while hundreds of fit men loafed about the camp because they were smart shirkers.

The food was neither attractive nor plentiful and this also led to deceit by old hands who brazenly paraded twice for each meal.

Jack was a happy man when one day he was paraded with a hundred others and told that they were a draft for the front line. The Somme might be a bad place but at least it was clean.

CHAPTER 9

Jack returned to the Somme with mixed feelings. By now the main battle was being on the southern section of the front and in a northerly direction. The original British attack was on a roughly right-angled front, the corner of the angle being about Albert. Virtually the whole of the eastern attack, from Gommecourt to Albert, had been held up but fair success had attended the northerly attack to the east and south of Albert.

It was to Albert that Jack's draft found its way, via a reinforcement camp. After a night there they spent an extraordinary day and night in some dug-outs on a hillside behind Albert. Here, there was little or no authority. They were a mixed crowd. Some were from Jack's own battalion, mostly pre-July casualties. The others were from various regiments. Each man had a tin of bully beef, a tin of jam, a handful of Army biscuits and some tea and sugar. They spent the whole day searching for fuel, boiling water for tea and eating biscuits with jam and biscuits with bully beef.

Next morning they were marched into Albert. This was Jack's first impression of a town denuded of its inhabitants. The men's boots clattered over the cobbled roads and he wondered how long it had been since they were swept and how long since worn setts had been replaced. He read the signs over the shops and wondered if the stocks were still to be found behind the boarded windows. Half-wrecked houses fascinated him. Bedsteads stood out nakedly in bedrooms from which the roof and walls had been torn away by shellfire. Had people been sleeping there when the awful messenger arrived?

In the square, he was fascinated by the hanging Virgin. It was said that the war would be over when she fell but British engineers had put off the happy day by wiring her up. Jack wished someone would fetch her down but that would not satisfy the prophesy. This would have to be carried out by a shell.

From the way odd soldiers hurried through the square, Jack guessed that it was not a place of good reputation. His party wheeled into a street of cottages where the men were told to billet themselves. Jack and four of his companions chose one that seemed to have the soundest roof and the strongest walls. These would not stop much and they looked vainly for a cellar.

The afternoon was spent digging for potatoes in the garden. What sort of a man had set them? Who would have eaten them if there had been no Somme battle? They feasted royally on those sweet young potatoes.

Next morning, a captain in a famous North Country regiment arrived from the line. They paraded and he marched them into a quiet lane. Jack could not make him out at all. He was a keen soldier but he also seemed much of a fop. He told them that they were to join his regiment – a regiment that ranked with the Guards in his estimation and beside which all theirs were mere gangs of no account. He told them of its great traditions. Jack felt like asking what they had done on the First of July. He resented the implied suggestion of inferiority in his own regiment. At the same time, however, the officer showed a keen interest in the experiences of the draft men, which also took in Mons and Ypres.

Next day, the battalion came out of the line. They had had a rough time and many were mourning lost comrades. The draft was fallen in behind. They were nondescripts of no account yet. As they marched along they noticed two mounted officers disengage themselves from the head of the column. They sat their horses while the draft marched past. They were two splendid figures of men. The younger of the two was a handsome man with a frank, open face and the body of an athlete. The other was as tall but broader and much older. Hs face was tanned to a deep bronze. It did not need the monocle to stamp him an aristocrat nor the ribbons on his chest to identify him as an old soldier.

"Not a bad lot! Said the younger officer. "No, they're not bad boys" the other replied in a deep, kindly voice. Jack and his friends felt better for hearing that. It seemed that, to the people that mattered, they did count after all.

Dusk was falling when, hot and footsore, the arrived at one of those straggling French villages of a layout which troops hated to reach after tiring marches for no one knew who would get the farthest billet. Here, the draft was sorted out and Jack and one other found themselves separated from the new draft. They were told to report to C Company. Evidently, this company had suffered least in the recent fighting. Jack, by now wise to these things, concluded that the next time they went in they would get the worst job.

They reported to C Company's sergeant major, a large veteran with a chest full of medal ribbons. In an even larger voice he handed them over to a platoon sergeant and they were shown into a barn. They were throwing off their packs when a voice in the doorway bawled "Shun." Every man sprang to his feet. Silhouetted against the light in the doorway was the aristocratic officer, still wearing his monocle. Obviously he was the Colonel and his younger companion had been his adjutant.

"All right, boys" he said. "I hope you will be comfortable, you've earned it. Tomorrow I will arrange hot baths for you. He smiled encouragingly and was gone.

"Who is he?" queried Jack of his neighbour. "That's old Bobbie – the Colonel – the finest man that walks. He's a Lord and a real gent. He never steps inside the officers' mess until he's visited every billet. And he's as brave as they make them in the line."

This reply was delivered in a strong North Country accent that Jack found difficult to understand. The meaning was clear, however. These rough fellows really worshipped their aristocratic chief. In return he came as near to loving them for their hardihood as ever a colonel could. It was this mutual respect in men so dissimilar in nature that made a splendid fighting unit.

As French villages went this one was a clean and bright affair and Jack enjoyed strolling among the peaceful cottages watching the locals and listening to the sounds of village life. Around tea-time, there was great excitement and Jack was informed that a pay-out was imminent. He wondered what his luck would be for, since he had left his unit, he had lived on charity. Married men would get five francs, single men ten.

Often, married men got nothing and this was a real grievance which dated back to 1914. In the first weeks of the war, the married men were mistakenly paid the full shilling a day whereas half should have been deducted and paid direct to their wives. The result was that debts were incurred and, even after this long passage of time, documents were handed out periodically showing the state of the debt. When a man was in debt he was not supposed to receive full pay. It struck Jack immediately that there must be something wrong about the business of men still paying 1914 debts in 1916.

The pay-out was the usual affair. A supercilious officer sat at a table, the sergeant major stood by him and the company quartermaster sergeant sat opposite. A man marched up. Clicked his heels, saluted, received his pay, signed the acquittance roll, saluted again and turned about. Nine out of ten grasped the few francs and, still in a state of excitement signed the roll without knowing what they had signed for. An unscrupulous CQMS could have cheated them out of hundreds of francs at every pay-out.

As a special concession, the two draft men were included in the pay-out. Normally, men were not paid until some official communication had been received to show the state of their accounts. Jack imagined the concession was due to the fact that they were both single and therefore not likely to be in debt.

As soon as he had signed his name, Jack was pulled on one side by the sergeant major and told to wait. He wondered what unconscious sin he had committed. Perhaps he had offended against regulations of which he knew nothing. He was still wondering when pay-out finished. "What's your name?" demanded the CSM. Jack told him. "What's your job in civilian life. Can you do clerical work?"

"It all depends what it is. I am not a clerk." said Jack. "I want you to try", said the sergeant major. "Report to my billet tomorrow."

On his return to the barn, Jack found that the news had preceded him. He was greeted with serious faces. "Don't take it on" one said. "The young fox has got the books into such a mess that he is funking the job and now you will get pushed into the mire".

Jack never found out what these company books were but he felt doubtful. Still, he reflected, he had no option. Refusal, even if it had been possible, would not have made him popular.

By the time he had found a cosy estaminet, sipped a cup of coffee and consumed a packet of biscuits – his first expenditure from his pay - dusk was falling. He was tired and he decided to lay his bed. He had a couple of blankets and he laid them out on a raised part of the floor beside another fellow who had already turned in, his valise at the head for a pillow. His neighbour, a big, lanky and rather untidy youth with an unprepossessing but not unpleasant face, informed him that he came from a village quite near Jack's home town. It was good to hear someone talk of the old places.

At about ten o'clock there was a new excitement. "Rum issue" said his new friend, reaching for the lid of his billy-can. "I don't take rum often" said Jack.

Eyes wide with amazement, his billy-can held at a ludicrous angle, the lanky youth looked as if he had been shot. "You'll never be short of a pal in this mob", he said. "Don't tell anyone. Draw it and bring it back to me".

The rum issue was a solemn rite. Two candles were produced and stuck side by side on an upturned box. The sergeant came in with a billy-can filled with the nut-brown liquid. By the look on the men's faces Jack guessed that any one of them would have fought the sergeant for the contents if the others had not been there. He produced a large spoon and, in complete silence, carefully measured out three spoonfuls per man. In every case, the recipient watched the process like a cat, lest the spoon should not be filled to the brim, received the liquid in his billy-can and went off into a corner to enjoy it. Jack took his place in the queue and later surreptitiously handed his share to the overjoyed youth.

This excitement over, another made its appearance. Cards were produced, a stump of candle was placed on a box and play began. The players squatted on their haunches while others knelt behind and watched. Gambling, Jack was to learn, was inbred in these men. They shuffled and dealt in feverish haste. One candle-end finished, a man went to his kit and produced another. Once a player was skinned another took his place at the box. Jack was fascinated by the intent look on their faces. It was midnight at least before he fell asleep and still the gambling continued.

More than once, during the remaining hours of darkness, he awoke but the gambling went on and he could hear the clink of coins, the rustle of paper money and the shuffling of cards. The last time he awoke, dawn was breaking but the game went on. He was told that it would continue the following night until the whole of the party's pay was won by one man. He would than stand treat for the others until the money was exhausted. In this way, the men had all the excitement of the game yet no one was much worse off in the long run. Between games, no one had any money except the winner unless they borrowed it, yet they spent most of their evenings in the estaminet.

That second morning Jack was complimented by the platoon officer on his clean rifle, a fact which to some extent restored his self-confidence. Immediately after the parade he reported to the sergeant major. From this interview he gathered that the clerical work required of him was really trifling. Before pay days he had to prepare the acquittance rolls from the company register which he also had to keep, prepare parade slates and, when in the line, report casualties. He also had to send in periodical reports on the wind for gas alarm purposes and on the situation regarding shelling. He was a little dismayed to find that the supercilious captain was the one to whom he presented the reports for signature.

The sergeant major told Jack not to worry about the captain. "But what about the company books?" he asked, with the warnings of the men in mind.

"These are the only ones we have" was the reply. Jack then realised that, in their ignorance, the men, had built up a great deal of mystery. The duplicates of the acquittance rolls were really in a frightful mess but Jack could see at once that no responsibility for previous errors could possibly devolve on to his shoulders. In any event, the responsibility was that of the quartermaster sergeant. He, like the others, was a miner, so it was essential for someone to give him a hand. While both he and the sergeant major were excellent fellows on the soldiering side of their work, it was painful to watch their clerical efforts.

Talking to the sergeant major in the privacy of his billet, Jack began to realise that he was not at all a bad fellow. He assumed his gruff manner to hold the rough lot of men he had to control. In reality, he was a homely man who thought the world of a wife and daughter in England. Jack felt that if he used a little tact he could get on well with him.

"You had better bring your kit along here" he was told. "In future you will sleep and eat in my billet. You will parade with the others. In the line there won't be much difference but you will miss fatigues and working parties." Jack was an old-enough soldier to understand what this meant.

Of course, he would be cut off from the companionship of the men but, though he might learn to appreciate these men for their courage and utter selflessness in things that mattered, he could see that anything like close friendship would be impossible. The cost of the job, a few minutes writing, would be a pleasant diversion.

76

When he returned with his kit, he met the sergeant major's batman, a rosy-cheeked, shy lad whose main job in life was to turn out the sergeant major as a sergeant major should be turned out and to see that his food was cooked a little more appetisingly. This was another pleasant surprise for Jack for it meant more and better rations. He also learned from the batman that the captain was a wealthy man who always had large supplies of food from Fortnum and Masons and the rich man's crumbs often fell on the sergeant major's table. Three more happy days were spent in this haven of rest and then orders came that the battalion would serve up the line.

It was a hot, sultry morning when they moved off. Jack's thoughts were busy. He remembered a staff officer saying that he would not see any more of the war, yet now they were in for it again. Going into the line on the Somme was never a light matter. You never knew what would happen before you came out again. It might be an attack or you might catch a counter attack. It was always sure to be rough. How would he behave in this new battalion? He had never been in action before except alongside his friends. A man liked to feel that if anything happened to him he had a friend by his side who would write to his folks. Here, his only link was the lanky youth who, in any case, had no idea of his home address. He was very conscious too of the earlier address by the captain and of the reputation of this unit. Could he fit in? On the other hand, he knew he had done his job on the First of July and that his unit had behaved as well as the regular troops in the vicinity.

He listened eagerly to the remarks passed by the men and tried to visualise the trenches they knew and which one they were marching to. It was a new world for him. His old friends were all men of fairly good education. These men had forgotten most of what they had learned at school, yet they had a rude but very sound vein of common sense. They also had a sense of humour which was keen and entertaining, if a little coarse.

His nearest neighbour, the batman, had nothing much to say but, on the march, Jack was always ready to listen rather than entertain. While he had never fallen out on a march, he still believed in conserving all the strength he had for it would have been a sad blow to his pride to have had to admit defeat.

Marching was never easy in hot weather. Recently, there had been no bread issue. The commissariat seemed to have fallen back on biscuits while the

Somme battle was in progress. These army biscuits were doubtless very good – they were believed to have great nourishing qualities – but Jack had always noticed that when marching on biscuits men always perspired more freely. This also happened when they drank heavily and he deduced from this that it was the effect of weakness.

Today, as he tired, he glued his eyes on the sunburned necks in front of him. They were the lean, angular necks of hard-worked men. He guessed that their owners could work hard in all kinds of positions in the mine. Long before army training, men like these had worked off any superfluous flesh they might have had. Today, their necks glistened with perspiration. They were not a bad lot on the march. Indeed, they were proud of their marching record. Jack guessed that they would not normally be walkers as his friends had been and he imagined that there had been some sore feet in the early days of their training.

They were also men who would bear pain rather than give in and he believed them when he was told that they never fell out unless sick. On the whole, they were not nearly as tall as his friends but they were sturdy and broad-shouldered.

The ten-minute halts came round with the usual hourly regularity. It was at these halts he learned that these men were careless of instructions. If they wanted a drink or a smoke they stole it. Rules to them were made to be broken and they had no fear of the consequences. No officer could prevent secret drinking. For his own part, Jack had disciplined himself against drinking on the march for the simple reason that he was better without it and he knew it was impossible to quench a marching thirst. The men who drank most always perspired most.

Down the long, straight, camouflaged road they dropped into Albert. During the summer every approach to Albert reminded Jack of the backwoods. There were still sufficient buildings for it to resemble a town. Indeed, the innumerable huts and camps gave it the appearance of a mushroom town in the wilds. There was also much hurried activity of men and vehicles. Add to that the picture of sunburned faces and the white bandages of the wounded and you have Albert.

Away up on the ridge on the German side of the town, irregular white lines wound about the hillsides showing where the chalk had been raised to the surface in trenching, thus advertising the location of the old front line trenches. Ambulances were always busy, flitting backwards and forwards, even old horse ambulances and there were always hundreds of walking cases. At night, fires were lit, some right on the skyline; such was the disdain of the advancing British Tommy for the enemy. Turbaned Indians who rarely spoke a word added to the picturesqueness of the scene, if one could see anything picturesque in what had recently been a bloody battleground.

A halt was called and the men filed into a field just outside the town for food and rest. Three hours later the move to the line began. By this time the traffic on the roads had become so dense that halts were frequent and utter weariness was the result. It was commonly believed among the men that this process of tiring them into utter desperation was a deliberate policy to make them careless of results. At any rate, it had that effect. Tempers were frayed and grousing increased.

Albert was soon left behind and the way led by ruined houses and old trenches, in all of which were relics of the fighting: battered steel helmets, broken rifles, shell cases and corpses. They entered a ruined village where a huge pile of debris showed the position of the church. There was an eerie feeling about this village. What lay beneath these piles of debris? It was strange to think that German troops had occupied it comparatively recently. A year or so earlier the villagers had walked in its lanes. Even now, peasants' treasures might be hidden under the houses. Long afterwards some people did go back and dig up their fortunes.

Jack's battalion had played a heroic part in the capture of this village and during halts he heard men discussing the fight. They had apparently been led through a heavy barrage on the fringe of the village. The men had set off in Indian file, with Colonel Robbie leading. Shells fell all around and it seemed marvellous that no one was hit. right" said one of the men to Jack. "When owld Robbie is in front we are all right".

It had been a quarter of a mile from where they were to the heads of the column but such was their faith in the CO that they had no fears. This blind faith was the most extraordinary thing that Jack had come across. It also seemed particularly odd for such rough men to have such regard for such an aristocratic individual. However, they did reach their trench without loss of any kind, although a long-distance shell had killed two drivers and four transport horses.

The trench they manned was beaten almost out of recognition. Filled up in places, parapets blown away in others, it provided little shelter. Here and there a man's leg stuck out of the wall of the trench, or a dead arm beckoned. Everywhere there seemed to be wires – old German wires and hastily-laid British ones. No one must touch them or they might cut the wrong ones. As it was, men stumbled over them and cursed the engineers. By a strange misfortune, the wires were thickest at the shallowest parts of the trench, where a man was supposed to run the sniper's gauntlet. The danger of such places was illustrated by the number of bodies lying about. They were nearly all khaki-clad bodies. What had happened to the field grey?

Jack's final position was in a former communication trench that had become a firing trench during the battle. So like a dog-fight was the Somme that it was not uncommon for the British to get into a trench that was still partly held by the Germans, the opponents being kept apart through the activities of bombers.

The Germans fought for every inch on the Somme and the British advanced literally inch by inch. Often, when an attack failed, a new trench would be dug under the noses of the Germans until the objective was finally taken. All over the front, bits of trenches were held which were within bombing range of each other.

That kind of thing probably accounted for the fact that after the war it was found that German casualties were nearly as high as our own. It said a good deal for the quality of the troops on both sides for, indeed, the Somme armies were the pick of the two nations.

CHAPTER 10

It was no picnic in this trench. Generally speaking it was proof against rifle fire but little else for continued shelling had made it wider and shallower. Jack was one of the first sentries posted. Shelling was pretty hot at the time but most of it seemed to be falling a little to his right. That sentry-go was memorable in his wartime career for a little gesture of friendship which gave him an insight into the character of the men of his new battalion.

He was gazing intently at the front, not at all sure of the location of the enemy trenches, when he started at a touch on his arm. "All right, sonny?" said the man. "Yes, thanks", said Jack. There was no explanation of the gesture and the man went on to talk of other things. Apparently he was regarded as of softer clay than these men and they wondered how he would be taking things. It was one of any number of such generous acts that were to make his association with these men a worthy experience.

A few minutes later a stretcher-bearer came along. This was also intended as a friendly act. It was remembered a week or two later when he was killed as he hurried over the top in a daylight attack to help the injured. A week earlier he had won the Military Medal.

Soon after he had finished his sentry duty Jack heard that four men had been buried by one of the shells he had been watching. It had dropped right in the trench. Digging uncovered only pieces of equipment.

The night passed fairly quietly. Towards dusk next evening, orders were issued that the men were to move along the trench to a section that was very much nearer the enemy line. This was the beginning of a most exciting night. The men who were being relieved made no effort to hide their haste. Jack thought things did not look too good. The two streams of men struggled past each other. Word was passed down repeatedly that their bombers were to return but no one took the slightest notice. Jack gathered that he was almost by a spa, for the possession of which a fierce fight had already been in progress for two days and nights. He could hear the rapid fire of machine guns and the bursts of bombs.

In the sap, Tommies and Aussies were mixed up. Two other units besides Jack's battalion had been in this sap. Orders were passed down requiring all bombers in the sap at the double. Then C company Lewis gunners were ordered to the sap. The energies of the whole battalion were soon to be centred on this sap, where a grim struggle was being fought by comparatively few men.

The Germans rallied and forced the British troops back 20 yards but the reverse only increased their determination. There was a call for more ammunition but none was available. The CO, who had taken charge of the sap operations, ordered every man to pass down his two spare bandoliers of SAA. The men stripped off their bandoliers and passed along the line. Parties hurried to the dump for more. Additional bombs were requested for a counter attack.

B company bombers to the front. Tight-lipped men passed down the line. "Good luck, Jimmy", "Good luck Hinnie" (a northern expression) were the greetings of Jack's new friends. One huge fellow – one of those shy men who appear to be half-ashamed of their stature – hove into sight. He was a policeman in peacetime. In the army he was a noted bomber. He ambled along, grinning sheepishly. Before 24 hours had elapsed, he had won a DCM. He was a man of tremendous strength, something that was to mean much to the sap fighters that night. The Aussies were to recall his feats for years afterwards, for he threw bombs continuously for 24 hours.

The counter-attack regained the lost 20 yards and carried the British another few yards ahead. More ammunition was demanded. The Germans could be seen massing for a counter-attack. Jack tried to picture the fight that was taking place so near. He was glad he was not in it. At the same time, he would have given anything to be in at it. This was real War – war in earnest.

Wounded were passed along on stretchers; some were crying out with pain. Others lay as if dead. Jack wondered when it would be his turn. The stretchers were carried as carefully as possible but it could not be helped that the men were shaken a bit. As yet, there were none of his unit. One young Australian, his arm dangling uselessly, asked for a cigarette. "It's hell up there, but it's good fun. The trouble is, there's no room to move. I was sitting on a dead man when I was hit. That big fellow you sent up is a marvel. He throws bombs like a demon".

More bombs were demanded. Take them out of the boxes, bend the pins together and push them along in sandbags. The bombers had no time to take them out of the boxes and nip the pins. They wanted them ready to throw. Fortunately, the fatigue party had returned and boxes of bombs sped down the line.

By this time, everybody was in a reckless mood. The call "Catch Hinnie" announced a sandbag of bombs hurtling along the trench. No one seemed to consider that the pins might come out altogether. Everyone was thinking of the men in the sap. More ammunition alternated with more bombs. The cries went on through the night and more wounded were passed down. News of the fight was gleaned from those less badly injured. Nearly all were full of the deeds of the policeman. In the charges he was always first out and there was no wonder the Germans gave way.

Next morning, the net result – fighting had ceased temporarily – was a gain of about 30 yards for the British. How many times that sap was fought over no one would ever tell but it must have been drenched in blood. So it was with many a trench on the Somme.

For Jack, it was one of the most hectic nights of his experience yet he had never fired a shot or seen an enemy bayonet. It was an almost uncanny feeling, to be so near a fight, guessing what was happening and then hearing confirmation from the wounded. At the same time, everyone had been so busily engaged that no thought of personal danger entered a man's head. Fortunately, casualties had been light except in the sap.

It was broad daylight when a relieving unit arrived and the battalion moved back to the old trench near the ruins of Colincamps.

Jack and the batman were despatched ahead to make preparations. To Jack's amazement, they were only a couple of hundred yards down the trench when the batman jumped out and made away over the open. It was a risky job for they were well within sniping range but obviously he could do no other than follow. Although they escaped the attention of snipers they had not gone far before the German gunners began to chase them with overhead shrapnel. The shell burst with a nasty clap in a white core of hot smoke and, for a few minutes, life was very hectic. They broke into a run and Jack thought they were well clear when there was a vicious smack and over went the batman.

Nice mess I'm in, though Jack. Then the batman's voice came up: "Are you all right? What hit me?"

"Aren't you hurt?" gasped Jack in relief. "No, but I bet my bully tin is burst" came the reply.

The shrapnel had struck right in the middle of the batman's pack, and they picked it out from between there and his tunic, where it had burned a hole. For the moment, however, they kept up their headlong flight to a place of comparative safety.

The matter was soon driven from their minds and, when Colincamps was left behind, they were proceeding merrily down the road without a care in the world. Their peace of mind was rudely shattered when two heavy howitzers roared out. The noise of the guns was followed by an ear-splitting explosion right above them, followed by a terrific rattling, as if an ironmonger's shop was falling to pieces on the road at their feet.

"Lucky miss, that," said the batman, gazing down at a huge piece of shell-case as big as a bucket and nearly an inch thick. "What was it?" asked Jack. "Just another piece of premature Yankee ammunition, I expect. Another yard nearer and we should have been no more. Fancy being shaved with that. We had better get a move on in case they have another".

They did.

The battalion spent another night in the old trench below Colincamps. Next day they had plenty of time to look about them. There seemed to be continual activity on some parts of the front, particularly in the direction of Puisieux and again over high Wood. There was something sinister about the wood, even in the distance. Not a Tommy on the Somme but knew of the terrible hand-to-hand fighting that had taken place beneath its once-peaceful trees and amongst its once-sunlit glades. The trees now were gaunt skeletons, stunted by explosives and splintered by shrapnel.

At night, large working parties were detailed off. Jack felt rather like a truant when the parties moved off for he was left behind, alone. As the night bombardments intensified he began to wish he was with his pals, even though a heavy barrage seemed to be falling in the direction which they had taken. He drifted towards the officers' dug-out, to which the sergeant major had adjourned.

Several shells fell dangerously near and an invitation to come down the stairs would have been welcome. Still, it was something to be able to hear voices. The sergeant major had not forgotten him (though, of course, he could not invite him down) and kept calling up to ask the state of affairs. Finally, when one shell fell so near that he felt the blast, he was called down and told to sit on the stairs.

It must have been past two o'clock when he heard feet clattering along the trench and dashed up to find six men of his own company. Sweating and cursing, they staggered down the trench. From their story it appeared that the party had only just begun digging when the barrage got them. At first they carried on but finally they had been withdrawn and told to split up and get back in small parties. They thought that casualties would be heavy but knew of none.

Gradually, the others made their appearance and it was found that only six were missing. These were dead. Night bombardments often gave rise to exaggerated reports. Not that the six deaths were of no consequence but first reports and spoken of many more.

During two further nights of working parties Jack spent his time watching the bombardments and soon knew the points at which most activity could be expected.

On the fourth afternoon orders to return to the line were received. The move began in daylight. It was surprising what chances were taken on the Somme yet daylight moves often proved least costly.

The fact was that, for most part, the fighting on the Somme was closing in. Apart from occasional long-distance shelling, troops outside a narrow belt enjoyed comparative immunity. Often men took to the open when not more than a quarter of a mile from trenches in which fierce fighting was taking place. This despite the fact that, at this period, both side still had plenty of efficient snipers. Jack knew several places that were made really deadly by snipers.

This particular relief went all night until the way led over a ridge that was in full view of the Bosch Hinterland. Indeed, from it could be seen green fields of corn. Before they reached this ridge the men could see that 5.9's were falling on it thick and fast and they appeared to be dropping just where the men had to pass.

It is not a particularly enjoyable sensation running the gauntlet of 5.9's – especially when one cannot estimate to a nicety when the next will fall, but a stretch of about 50 yards of open ground had to be covered. Jack and the batman were unlucky when their turn came. They were just in the middle when the warning boom of the guns sent them down to earth. The scream of the shells was drowned in a deafening roar. They gave themselves up for lost. Dirt splattered all over them and for one breathless instant they waited for the searing shrapnel.

"Come on" yelled the batman and they dashed for the trench and its sheltering walls, only just in time.

The position taken up was in support and a miserable night was spent. The front was alive with shelling and, to add to the discomfort the district was drenched with tear gas. Sleep was impossible, so irritated were the eyes. Then word came to move up to the attack. The batman had been detailed off to go with a water party. Jack missed his company. A generous rum ration was given out and the batman's issue was carefully covered and left in his funk hole. He never drank it for he was on his way to Blighty, wounded.

A narrow slit of a trench was occupied and the news filtered through that a German trench that had withstood two attacks was to be taken at all costs. Very easy to say it, thought Jack. However, there was only 50 yards to go and the defence had weakened.

The attack was a big success but only a few prisoners were taken. It was an old story on the Somme. When the Germans realised that we had set our minds on gaining a trench they left a few men to keep up a pretence and then retired to a new position. Still, the success straightened out the line ready for the next attack. It would long be remembered by Jack as his first attack since 1 July but the experience restored his confidence, which had been badly undermined by the previous disaster.

The next day they handed over to a new unit and marched back to Albert. Here, Jack had his first experience of the benefits of living with the sergeant major. It was dark when they arrived at one of the empty houses but the CQMS had candles burning and a fine meal, including a ham from the Captain's private commissariat. The tea was nectar. Albert was heaven after the line and, as he stretched his weary limbs after the meal, Jack felt that, after all, it was very good to be alive. He lay drowsily listening to the CSM, the CQMS and another old soldier, the QMS, yarning of previous campaigns. When he slept, he dreamed of his Vision.

Albert was a much healthier place by now but one night a long-distance shell fell on a house nearby and killed two of the Brigade staff.

The next day a fresh battalion of Aussies moved up to the line. They were a fine, devil-may-care lot, but they were tired and swearing. Somehow, however, Jack thought they looked as if the heat did not bother them half so much as it did him and his friends. He liked the look of their lean figures and imagined they were hardened before they began training. They looked more than a match for anything they would meet and they proved it. Poperinghe was a hard nut but they made it their own. Not, however, until there had been some of the fiercest fighting of the war between those sunburnt men and the finest German troops that could be found. Gradually, inch by inch, they fought their way to the windmill and Mouquet Farm.

There was something that touched a responsive chord in watching troops from different parts of the Empire moving up to align themselves alongside English troops. Who could tell what associations some of these might have with one's home or friends. Jack had already experienced similar thoughts during his recent stay in hospital.

There was something that never failed to touch him in the thought that the bony Highlander might hail from some cottage where a fond mother watched every day as the postman made his way across moorland; or that big Canadian who might have heard the call from a log hut in the wild North; or that fresh-faced boy with the wide hat who would have been more at home raising sheep in far-away New Zealand.

Then there were these Australians. Jack was always trying to judge whether they were raw English immigrants or descendants of the old convicts. Some of them looked hard enough to be the latter and they were tough fighters. They were outspoken, too, on the merits of British Tommies. They did not fail to criticise when criticism was due – not least worthy of criticism in their view being the old frontal attack generals. But they appreciated even more warmly than they criticised. They were great pals with Jack's unit.

It was raining next time Jack's battalion moved up. They had to occupy a broken-down support trench. Jack never spent a more miserable night. He had a bad attack of neuralgia and crouched beneath a sheet of corrugated iron, wet through and miserable. Tot after tot of rum failed to bring relief.

Next day, some comedian of a quartermaster sent up a quarter of fresh beef. It was decently buried since there was no possibility of cooking it. Bully beef was more suitable but, when Jack opened his, it was sagging about in the tin, so hot had the day become. They moved up for another attack that night but it was called off and they moved back to Scots Redoubt, a series of old German dug-outs.

Scots Redoubt was Jack's first introduction to the strong defences that the Germans had enjoyed in their old positions and gave him his first idea of the magnitude of the task the British had set themselves on 1 July. This redoubt was a work of the tunneler's art, consisting of a wonderful network of tunnels capable of holding large numbers of men. It was only one of a number, he was told, and it demonstrated in no uncertain way why the capture of the German trench system had been so costly.

Another thing it emphasised was the difference between the two armies engaged. The early school of British officers still, at this time, dominated the councils of the British army and scorned shelter. Brave men themselves, for the most part, they loved the frontal attack and hated to feel that the British soldier needed to be sheltered from the modern means of warfare. Dug-outs were practically taboo in the British lines. It was believed that they would destroy the morale of the men. The result was that the British army suffered thousands of unnecessary casualties.

That there were some grounds for this attitude Jack knew full well. Troops called upon to emerge from safety in a dug-out came into the open half-dazed and inclined to be nervous. But they did come out whole and a whole man, even though he might be shaken a bit, could man a trench and hold up an attack. That was the reason why the German trenches were so strongly manned on 1 July, even though they had been blown about by a week's bombardment. The bombardment had passed harmlessly over their heads.

Thiepval was further proof of this and it was said that the British had had to use armour-piercing shells to get down to the tunnels there. The village Jack's unit had attacked was equally strong – indeed, in postwar days, it was described as a mine of iron, so much British ammunition had been poured into it in an endeavour to break into its underground strongholds. At Thiepval, it took long weeks, which dragged into months, to subdue the sheltered garrison.

The capture of the German first line positions introduced the British to numbers of these underground fortresses. Some were lit by electricity; others had trolley systems on rails to convey the wounded. Naturally, the British Tommies made some very pointed comparisons and British authorities and engineers suffered in the comparison. A man who had lain out through a winter expecting that his opponent had had a similar experience was not likely to relish the knowledge that he had been living in comparative leisured ease.

Much of this was conveyed to Jack by the new batman. Dave was a great character. A big, strong-headed youth, his face was as ugly as his disposition was kind. Since leaving school, he had worked down a mine. He knew what it was to hack and hew in all kinds of uncomfortable positions. He was used to the sight of blood and fractures. Absolutely fearless, he was as cool a customer as a man might ever hope to find. On one occasion, it was said, he dug out with his bare hands, six men who had been buried by a shell. The barrage had been so heavy that the rest of the party stampeded, but Dave stayed and, nails broken, fingers lacerated, he tore away at the earth until the last man was in a position to breathe freely. He then summoned stretcher-bearers and superintended the removal. Later, he explained his broken nails by explaining that he had had a fall. He received no honour for no one knew the story until, months later, one of the men returned from hospital.

CHAPTER 11

Dave the batman was a jewel. Not that he was particularly careful when cleaning boots or buttons. Indeed, in that department he was rather weak. Personally, he was rather untidy, like his shock of hair. It was not that he was afraid of work. He would polish with great vigour but one had to watch that he did not leave a patch of Soldier's Friend behind. The CSM soon gave up hope of making him tidy. No one on Earth could have done that.

In the line, however, his ingenuity was unsurpassed. He had already proved to Jack that he could mash a bully tin of tea if he had only the water and a bit of pull-through rag soaked in rifle oil. He had no fear of King's Regulations, GRO's or anything else. The King was a long way off and so were headquarters. Neither of them could see what he was doing in the line. Hence the frequent misuse of equipment and supplies. The pull-through patent heater was a remarkable invention for if a Tommy only had a drink of tea nothing else on Earth mattered.

Dave was also a man of few words. He rarely strung more than half a dozen together and when they came you were lucky if you understood them. There were two reasons for this. One was his broad North Country accent and the other the peculiar work of his mind, which made it difficult to guess what he was likely to say. He had been in Scots Redoubt soon after it was taken and he described a peculiar incident.

As Jack knew full well, the ground was pretty sticky on 1 July, though that particular day turned out hot. In the fighting here a huge Highlander met an equally big German. The two must have lunged together. They died together, bayonets thrust home and in such a manner that both remained standing, their feet anchored in the sticky mud. (Whenever the author visits the battlefields in these post-war years and sees the Highlander memorial to the 51st Division, his mind recalls this incident, which was pictured so clearly by the batman Dave).

Dave pulled Jack out of many a bad scrape on the Somme. He was always the same – cooler in action than at any other time and he seemed to have a bent for doing the right thing. He could always pick the best way to avoid barrages and his sense of location was uncanny. On the darkest night he seemed able to find places even though he had only seen them once.

During the Somme struggle the British Tommy had much to contend with. The German shelling was heavy and the German soldier was fighting as at no other time for the simple reason that it was the Somme that first turned his invincible German army on to the defence. There was also the definite inferiority of the guns that were available to the British. It was not an uncommon thing for British trenches to be made untenable by British guns. More than once, Jack had seen British companies blown out of their trenches by British guns.

Reference has been made to the difficulties due to trenches being only partly captured and so obstinate were both sides that often it obtained for days that the British would hold one part of a trench and the Germans the other. In this ding-dong battle communication trenches, switchlines and all kinds of saps were temporarily converted into front line trenches. This state of affairs naturally caused the gunners some trouble but the main difficulty was due to the guns they were using and the ammunition they were firing. Bad ammunition caused prematures, which were deadly things. Sometimes guns would burst, sometimes the shell came only a few yards from the gun and then blew back, wiping out the gun teams. Sometimes the shell came just far enough to explode on our own infantry.

More often the trouble was due to bad or worn rifling. Shortage of guns meant that they were used for much longer than they should have been. This meant worn rifling, leading to shell falling short.

There were some things that even a long-suffering Tommy just couldn't stand. One was the thought of munition workers for, apart from the fact that it was human nature to envy the much-pampered man who had sought shelter in a munition factory, Tommy never got it out of his head that the munition workers were letting him down by their strikes and their scamped work. Therefore, short shelling made Tommy see red. He would blast and fume. His officers would turn the telephone wires to the batteries red hot but the cool reply would always be a blank denial. It seemed impossible to make gunners realise that, even if the sights were set right, shells were not going where they were aimed. Jack had experience of this time and time again. More than once he was the runner who was sent back to report matters.

On one memorable occasion he had to pass down a battered trench when he came to a particularly hot sniping corner. "You can't get past there, son", said an artillery observer lying full length across the trench. "There's bodies all round".

"But I must get past" replied Jack, all hot and bothered. "Well, the last three got it in the napper", was the reply. "Can't you see the trench is filled in and you've got to bring yourself in full view?"

"Anyhow, I shall have to try", said Jack, his heart sinking. He looked at the gap and at the stiff bodies and then he thought of his pals. "It's up to me anyway, so here's for it". He made a careful survey of the place, gave his slung rifle a jerk and dashed at the spot. He reached the highest point, believing he had made it, when his foot caught in some telephone wires. Something whistled past the back of his neck and he fell headlong into the deeper part of the trench at the other side. The fall probably saved his life. He called back to the observer. "What?" came the astonished reply. "I though he had got you".

Another of my nine lives, thought Jack cynically and he bustled on. At the artillery headquarters his message was torn open and the officer saw red. "You must be damn fools", said the OC. "We are firing on the German trenches in front of you".

"But you are not" replied Jack, beside himself. "The Germans aren't shelling yet we have had five killed and a dozen wounded; and we can hear them coming".

Jack could see that the officer was, for a moment undecided whether to curse him or to take notice. Fortunately, for Jack had overstepped the mark in his reply, he came round and agreed to look into the matter.

Jack did not take the short cut back. He thought it was enough to tempt providence once in a day and he took a roundabout route on the return journey. He had succeeded in his mission, however, and the shelling had ceased when he returned. The fact was, of course, that the artillery were so loath to lose a gun that they refrained from pulling out worn guns until new ones were available.

Tommy never took a keener interest in the activities of the air force than he did on the Somme. These humming birds were friends indeed. It was about this time that the British seemed to gain real supremacy in the air. Invariably, they drove the Germans off and so much were they held in awe by the enemy that German shelling was almost bound to cease if a British plane came over. Many a day, Jack and his pals suffering high casualties prayed for the approach of a British plane. More than once, the relief was so great that cheering broke out. After a long night, made weary by the uncertainty of life, the first aeroplane in the morning came like a Godsend. The knights of the air were very dear to the heart of the Tommy. He felt that they, at least, sympathised with his lot.

These nights on the Somme were hard. Overcoats were rarely taken up to the front line and, even in summer it is a cold job lying on the ground. Jack always kept a newspaper to take up with him. It took little room, added no weight and was quite useful to wrap around the legs.

Funk holes were common on the Somme. For the benefit of those who have never heard of them, they should be described. Most men had a horror of being hit in the stomach. Now when a man lay down in a trench at night – provided he was a healthy man like 99 per cent of the Somme British were – he would go to sleep. Most youngsters also sleep heavily. Jack could easily sleep through a bombardment, much to the horror of the CSM, who feared that he would be killed in his sleep. It was useless for Jack to remonstrate: the CSM persisted in waking him.

The point is that, when a man lay down to sleep he invariably turned his face to the front wall of the trench and hunched up legs and body, both for the purposes of warmth and to shield his stomach. The Germans were still using a lot of overhead shrapnel and the Tommy carried the protection of his stomach a step further by burrowing into the bottom of the trench wall, just sufficiently to crawl under. The funk hole was Tommy's shelter from shrapnel. Colonels were apt to get indignant about funk holes. They undermined the strength of the trench. Of course they did, but they also saved thousands of lives and, after all, Colonels don't need funk holes. Tommy thought funk holes were ideal for the moment and, as Colonels were not there at night-time, funk holes continued to be burrowed.

News of the advent of tanks soon spread among the rank and file, who thought at first that they were some Heaven-sent gifts to save the lives of Tommies in attack. It must be realised that the thinking Tommy always had at the back of his mind the enormous casualties when men had to cross the open in the face of machine guns. The exorbitant losses of 1 July – some said 100,000 though, of course, it is now known that 60,000 was the more correct figure – were repeated in proportion in nearly every attack. Every Tommy on the Somme had seen the barbed wire full of khaki bodies. There were occasional successes at a smaller price but the daylight attacks often insisted upon took a terrible toll. Naturally, then the Tommy who had seen many attacks was consumed with the idea that attacks with mere men could not succeed except with heavy losses.

A first-class battalion was no more immune than a third-rate battalion would have been and what successes were achieved were due to the outstanding bravery of a few determined men who got through.

It will be seen, then, that when stories filtered through that these new monsters, proof against bullets, had simply crushed the dreaded machine gun nests out of existence, Tommy was ready to believe and to cheer at the most outrageous stories. One day Jack walked a couple of miles behind a pair of these tanks – a male and a female, so-called because the male was armed with six-pounder guns and the female with machine guns. All the way the men walking up to them and stroked them as if they were animals capable of appreciating caresses. They looked on almost with reverence and the tank's inventors would have been awarded the Tommy's highest honour. So far as Jack was concerned, however, these hopes were followed by sudden and definite disillusionment.

One afternoon they were resting in a trench near the scene of the 5.9 episode, now safer because of a recent advance, when news came that Jack's unit was to continue the advance. In the dying daylight they gazed down on the village of M...(Morval?) with a new interest. Every yard of the intervening space was pock-marked with shell holes, a memorial to British gunnery. The village itself was black with bursting shells. It was not the habit of Germans to give up anything willingly and, when generosity was forced upon them, they made sure that the invaders had a warm time and that whatever shelter they had themselves enjoyed should be denied the new occupants. The village that evening offered a warm welcome to all and sundry. It was not an inviting sight. It seemed as if every living thing in such an inferno would be blown to atoms. It said much for the discipline of the young British soldier that he could be persuaded that his duty lay in such places.

Suddenly, across the evening air, there was the sharp crack of a rifle. "What's that?" demanded the CSM shortly. A moment later two men came along leading a white-faced third. "Rifle bullet in the arm, sir" said one, non-commitally. "How did it happen?" said the CSM, growing stern. The white-faced man told some story about cleaning his rifle when it went off. He deceived no one. Everyone knew that he must have been looking deep into the inferno in the village and that the spectacle had proved too much for his nerves. He was not, in any event, a first-class soldier.

"Who saw it" demanded the CSM, an edge in his voice that boded no good for the man. "Fetch the platoon sergeant". Try as they would, however, they could find no witness. The man was sent away under escort. He was covered in suspicion but no action was ever taken against him for casualties in the pending attack removed any possible witnesses.

The way down to the village led through a sunken road. It was a shambles, German and British dead lay everywhere. A bridge lay awry, twisted like a child's toy. There was an air of foreboding about that road. They were all glad to leave it behind.

Thud, crash, thud crash and heavy shells began dropping in quick succession. Each thud was followed by a splintering crash and the noise of falling debris. "Keep by me", muttered the stolid Dave. The pair were sent with four others into an old German dug-out right in the heart of the village. It seemed that all the shells were being aimed at that point. They reached it in a series of mad rushes. Time and time again the swish of an approaching shell sent them on to their faces but at last they tumbled down the entrance.

There must have been forty steps. Evidently there had been a dressing station here for the smell of dressings and bandages was sickening. They could only move about ten yards along the gallery before they came to a halt. "Fallen in, here" said Dave. "One of ours done it".

"What a horrible stench" said Jack. "There'll be German bodies under there, poor devils". None of the men felt over-happy about his surroundings though, as always with good soldiers, no one voiced his fears but rather pretended an artificial gaiety.

Each knew, however, that a dug-out once buried was quite likely to be buried again. The heavy shells now falling so near sounded as if they would break into any dug-out. They continued throughout the night. First, the noise of the express train rapidly coming nearer and then the horrible crump followed by the scattering of tons of debris. One's mind was in such a state that sleep was impossible for the shape of the gallery gave one the feeling of being caught like a rat in a trap. "I wonder how the rest of the boys are faring", said Dave, and Jack wondered too. It seemed as if they were cut off eternally from the others.

Morning came and they were still alive. At the first streak of dawn a messenger came to fetch them to the trench where the company was gathering. They moved along into a trench that was already occupied by another of their companies. It transpired that this other company, together with a second company of the battalion, were to attack. Half an hour after the attack opened the remaining two companies, including Jack's, were to move into a switch trench with a view to further exploiting the attack, if it succeeded.

Once that morning, Jack caught sight of the supercilious officer he had encountered on joining his new battalion. The thought of action seemed to have put new life into him. His eyes shone and his face was alight. One thing: the beggar isn't afraid, though Jack. He was not. He proved to be one of the coolest men in the battalion.

"Two tanks coming over with us" said one of the men. "Where are they?" asked Jack, ears and eyes wide open. "We don't attack until noon and they will only come up just in time. They moved into the sunken road during the night".

The faces of the men who were going over were tense. Many of them had pals in Jack's company. There were whispered consultations and little valuables changed hands. Jack knew what was happening and felt a little out of it. He knew none of these sufficiently well to be trusted with intimate things to be sent home. Like so many thousands of men who, day by day, took their lives in their hands on the Somme, these men knew that attacks could not be carried out without losses. It would have been a good thing for some of the fierce old warmongers at home if they could have seen these lads – in full joy of youth – calmly preparing for death and calmly making arrangements for the disposal of their belongings.

"The tanks will make short work of them", said Jack cheerfully. In his heart however, he had lost the early confidence that he had enjoyed when he first saw these two monsters. "I hope so", said another, "but I am not partial to these daylight attacks".

"It looks as if you have some dead ground at the beginning", said Jack.

"Yes, we shall reach the ridge and then I expect we shall get it".

The artillery was gradually increasing its power and, though a good length of the German trenches was targeted, it was only in front of Jack's battalion that the attack was to take place. The Germans were not yet retaliating.

One of his company stretcher-bearers came along. "Hello, Taylor" said Jack, you've put the ribbon up".

"Aye. I wish I hadn't". Taylor had been awarded the Military Medal the week previously and he now referred to the superstition in the battalion that the Military Medal men nearly always got it in the next engagement. "Oh, rubbish!" said Jack, "you jolly well deserved it".

"I'm not very happy about it, anyway". Suddenly he flushed and looked rather guilty. "Would you mind posting this note if – if anything happens?"

Jack's first impulse was to try to laugh off the incident but a glance at the other's face told him that this would cause serious offence. He temporised. "But you are not going over. It is only the other two companies".

"I know, but don't think I shall stay here when the wounded need help".

"No, of course not. I hadn't really thought because, on 1 July, stretcher-bearers were purposely kept back". Jack took the note, feeling the responsibility of a grave charge.

Shortly before the attack, the tanks lumbered and rattled into sight. Their advent simply turned the Germans stark, staring mad. BOS signals went up in showers. Even in the brilliant sunlight it seemed that every colour of the rainbow was represented. They brought a quick response from the German guns. It seemed as if every gun on the Somme was turned on that sector.

In the midst of it all, tight-lipped officers shouted "Over, boys" and, without hesitation, the men of the attacking waves leaped out of the trench. It seemed unreal to Jack to see these khaki figures going forward on this brilliant noon, and to think that now they were human beings capable of thought while, in a matter of minutes or seconds, many of them would be motionless, cold clay. At first, the steady line remained intact.

"Wait till they hit the rise" said Dave, with clenched teeth, his eyes fixed on the back of one of his home pals. A man dropped, hit by shrapnel. "Where are you going, Taylor?" The stretcher-bearer, heedless of everything, eyes fixed on the fallen man, was yards out of the trench. "Good lad, that" said Dave "but he knows he's marked. From that moment, Jack's whole attention was on the stretcher-bearer.

As the men neared the top of the rise a wave of lead swept them. The reaper's scythe, thought Jack. Dozens went down together. Taylor was not alone. A dozen stretcher-bearers followed him. "No chance, damn it" muttered Dave. "They can't do it. They've another hundred yards to go".

From the trench, nothing further could be seen of the attack. The wicked splutter of machine guns continued and every man who had faced machine guns felt himself flinching for those who were in the open. The stretcher-bearers could be seen, stooping as they ran from one prone figure to another. When they didn't stop Jack knew it was because they could do nothing. His eyes glued on Taylor, he saw him working like a Trojan but at last he ventured too far. Suddenly, the bowed figure doubled still further and fell. Jack knew Taylor was done. Something told him that he had received the fatal wound he had dreaded. He turned, a sob in his throat, but Dave had disappeared.

"His pal was hit and he's gone to fetch him", volunteered the next man. Jack turned again to the front. There was the shock-headed Dave rushing towards the rise. He was not bowed as the others had been but ran upright, heedless of bullets and shrapnel alike. Just on the rise he flung himself down beside one of the prone figures. He seemed to be talking to him, then he stood up. It seemed to Jack that he made a gigantic target as he stood against the skyline. Jack's heart stood still.

Unhurried, Dave bent down and gently picked up his pal, lifted him carefully over his shoulders and turned back.

He can't do it, thought Jack. Not that he thought Dave was not strong enough to carry the man. He knew that this rough lad, trained since boyhood in the mines of the north, could carry a man like a baby. But he felt sure he would be hit. There must have been sportsmen among the Germans that day for the reckless lad came safely back and handed his burden over to the stretcher-bearers. He took his place in the trench without a word but Jack though he caught the glisten of a tear. He had a woman's heart, this man, where others' hurts were concerned. No personal pain would have brought a murmur from his lips.

"Wonder what the tanks are doing" said Jack. "The machine guns are still firing".

"I don't know", replied Dave, a far-away look in his eyes. Doubtless in that moment his mind was far away in a northern pit village, for there was little hope his pal would go down the mine again. Also, these men married young and the wounded man had a wife and two children.

They had little time for reflection. Evidently expecting a further attack, the enemy guns were ranging their trenches. There was a sharp crack overhead followed by a hiss. A shrapnel fragment bedded itself into the trench wall, a foot from Jack's head. The CSM came hurrying along. "Keep down, boys, they're sending over shrapnel. We shall be moving along in a minute".

Shells were falling all about and great chunks of parapet were blown away. After one particularly deafening roar, Jack felt as though someone had hit his arm with a rifle butt. A stinging pain ran through him.

"By God, that's a whack. Let's look". Dave tore up Jack's sleeve. Blood was gushing out but it was clearly only a slight wound. "Lucky, but it'll be pretty stiff". They bound a bandage tightly about the arm.

They moved along to the switch, a narrow slit of a trench scarcely deep enough to walk upright. "Attack's a failure", someone said. Both tanks were smashed and useless. The supercilious officer burning to be in it had taken over forty men to try to retrieve the day. He had gone over merrily, swinging his cane.

Jack's second misfortune soon came. The German gunners must have seen them taking up the new position. Jack heard it coming.

It was a horrible feeling. He could not have moved even if there had been time. He felt like a rabbit fixed by a stoat. He could not budge. There was a terrific thud. He imagined he could feel hot air about his legs. A great weight descended on his ribs. Acrid fumes filled his lungs. He could not see. He could not breathe. A weight seemed to be pressing all about him. His first impulse was to struggle but he could not move a finger. How glad he was to catch first a glimpse of sunlight and then Dave's ugly face. Even in that moment he could not help noticing that Dave's face had lost its stolidity. It was full of expression, tenderness and fear lest he should find his friend dead, and straining with effort.

"Keep still. Don't struggle. You'll soon be free". His rough voice had softened. Evidently he feared that release might only reveal gaping wounds. He and three other were scratching at the earth like devils. Dirt flew in all directions before their frenzied arms.

"I'm all right", said Jack.

"Wait a bit, until we get you clear". Gradually the weight lifted. "It's good to breathe", he said, shakily. "Thanks, old man".

Dave looked uncomfortable. "I thought..." He did not finish the sentence and Jack followed his eyes to the two corpses lying in the bottom of the trench. "Same shell?" queried Jack.

Dave nodded. "Aye, you're lucky."

"A narrow shave" said the CSM, looking at the others. "Poor chaps".

Jack had said he was all right but he soon found that he seemed to have lost all control of his nerves. He was shaking like a leaf. With good reason, too, for burying was one of the nastiest experiences.

Dusk found half the company out on no-man's land. They believed in burying their own pals. Jack learned then of an incident which softened his memory of the supercilious officer. Evidently knowing the courage of his batman – a bright, fresh-faced lad still only 18 though he had been in the army over two years – he had sent him back to the reserve officer with a bogus message. He knew it was of no use simply telling him to stay in the trench. He would have followed his officer anywhere. Jack thought it was one of the finest things he could have done.

The shelling ceased towards evening but snipers kept busy. Yet the men kept at work in no-man's land and it was reported soon after dusk that all the wounded were in and that many of the dead were buried. The two companies were practically annihilated.

One strange, square looking chap in Jack's company set himself up as an undertaker, his objective being to mark each grave. He was clever with a jack knife and produced some very creditable crosses. From somewhere he procured some stakes and chipped out names and numbers on them.

"Here's one for Jack Smith", he mumbled, hacking away furiously. Another man slid over the top to put the cross in position. "I'll take Tommy Peterson's myself" said the square one. "I know his mother". He finished off the cross and straightened himself to mount the parapet. There was a sharp crack and he fell dead at Jack's feet, shot clean through the head.

At 9 o'clock another unit filed in to take over and Jack's battalion moved back to the trench of the 5.9 episode, but not before the others had promised to finish the burials. How badly they did it.

Clear of the line, the full story of the attack gradually came out. The tanks had mot merely failed to help the attack. They had proved a hindrance. Both had stuck half way over no-man's land and, so great was the German fear of these steel monsters that they had drawn a veritable hurricane of steel on to the unprotected infantry. Moreover, as was only natural, the men had tended to bunch in the shelter of the tanks and this had led to fearful casualties.

The last seen of the supercilious officer appeared to be that he had jumped into the German trench, still waving his men on with his gold mounted cane. This story was denied by some. He had been blown to pieces near the tanks, said one man. Another was equally certain that he had seen a German officer shoot the Captain. This emphasised the difficulty of assessing casualties. Deaths were usually known but it was common for the fate of a man to be the subject of conflict.

I saw him blown up, his steel helmet flew 40 yards" said one.
But I saw him go down with a machine gun bullet in his groin" said

another.

It was always the same and it was quite to be expected when the men were excited in an attack.

There had not been the slightest chance of success. Miraculously, due to their following a depression in the ground, Jack's company party had not suffered so heavily, but they had been in a hopeless position and the remnants retired.

Old Bobbie was heartbroken, not at the failure of the attack but at the loss of his boys, for whom he felt a real affection. When he crawled out into the open to watch the progress of the attack, his orderlies nearly fainted but they had to follow. He was as cool as a cucumber.

When the machine guns took their terrible toll, tears sprang to his eyes. "My poor lads, my poor lads" he groaned. Thus this scion of a noble house mourned the loss of brave collier lads. He was too good a soldier, obviously, to criticise those who had ordered the attack, but he would have something to say later.

The remnants of the battalion marched back in silence. For most, their thoughts were too deep to be uttered. It was one of the worst setbacks the battalion had had.

CHAPTER 12

The battalion's next gruelling was near L... (Le Transloy?), just preceding the capture of this village by two sister battalions. There was an ominous quiet that evening as the battalion moved up.

On the Somme there were always plenty of bodies about but there was something about the pose of the young Highlander who was lying in the open near a bend in the communication trench which compelled attention. He was a handsome, fair laddie and he lay there in the natural pose of sleep, his head resting on his left arm. It is one of those inexplicable things that, of all the hundreds of bodies a man saw, odd ones stand out in the memory.

Jack would never forget that handsome laddie from Scotland. Somehow, despite his natural attitude, he looked incongruous in this French landscape. He should have been sleeping by his sheep in the Highlands, with some proud mother preparing his evening meal while she dreamed of his future success. He would need no more of her delicious scones. She might dream on but her dreams would never be fulfilled. Her fate was the dreaded orange envelope, the quiet mourning in the cottage and the errant tears as she sat, still and thoughtful, in the village kirk.

Jack's company moved into a trench that had been occupied by a south country regiment. The term "had been" is used for there was no official handing over. The outgoing unit, like the bombers near P...... had evidently had enough. They ran like rabbits as soon as the first men of the new unit appeared. The hardy northerners looked on contemptuously. The experience of this particular battalion may have been unfortunate but they never had much faith in southern troops apart from those from London, marks of whose valour they had seen very definitely in places like High Wood.

No sooner were the men in position than orders were issued to deepen the trench. Evidently something had been said to the officers. The men obeyed with alacrity, for the night was quiet enough so far as the shelling was concerned.

The trench was soon deepened by another two feet. Trench digging was child's play to men who had delved in the bowels of the Earth. There was something uncannily ominous about the situation, however. As things settled down, strange cries broke the evening's stillness. "There must be some wounded still lying out", said Dave. The cries seemed to be coming from all directions, but mainly from the rear. "Doesn't say much for that mob that's just gone out". Just then the CSM came along.

"Seem to be some wounded out, sir", said Dave.

"Are you sure"?

Dave drew attention to the sounds. The CSM was a man of action. Soon, three parties had been made up. They slipped over the top like shadows. Half an hour passed and then Dave re-appeared. Jack was standing with the CSM.

"They are over to the left rear, sir" reported Dave. "In a kind of spinney. We have found six. They all seem to be pretty bad and we shall need stretchers. They are half-starved too because they've been out there for three nights".

Stretcher-bearers, assisted by the search parties, were busy half the night and the MO and his staff also had a busy time. The first streak of dawn showed that the wire in front of the trench was full of khaki bodies, spreadeagled on the barbs, some standing almost erect. Such scenes always affected Jack. In some parts the ground rose from the trench and men were sent out to bury the bodies.

All went well until about noon. Whether it was that the enemy's attention was attracted by the new earth thrown up during the night or whether it was the activity of the burying parties, no one could tell. Suddenly, however, the Germans opened an intense bombardment of the position.

The first thought was naturally one of thankfulness that the wounded had been safely removed. An ordinary bombardment was not treated with any particular respect by these men. Now it was the opening of a two-day bombardment that was to try the nerves of the hardest among them to the utmost.

Added to the usual high explosives were nasty overhead shrapnels which would, of course, have been harmless if there had been head cover but there was none in open trenches. Spitting whizz-bangs, which hit the parapet at the same moment that the noise of the gun met the ear, were also mixed in.

That afternoon, a man from the right section came hurtling along the trench, half-demented. A shell had buried half his section. Jack never heard what became of him. If ever there was a case of shell shock, this was it. He careered madly along the trench and no one attempted to stop him.

Casualties mounted high. A shell landed on the signal post, killing two and wounding two of the company signallers. More were requisitioned from another company but a second shell cleaned them up too.

What added to the gloom was that the ration parties failed to return. They had been wounded but, at the time, this could only be guessed by the besieged company. Contact with the outside world seemed totally denied. The shelling continued throughout the night and there was no respite the following day. That afternoon Jack, the CSM, a sergeant and two men were smoking in a fairly good traverse when a shrapnel shell burst right above them. The sergeant and one man were badly hit. The other man caught a Blighty and Jack noticed the CSM flinch. Jack alone escaped but the CSM was soon back from the dressing station. The MO had soon extracted the fragment and he felt it was his duty to return to the trench.

It was as well he did for the company badly needed its steadiest men. Some of the best men were showing signs of nerves. Dave, as usual, was a tower of strength, heartening the waverers and helping carry out the wounded. Jack would never forget the night when a corporal twice his age, a sturdy, black-bearded man who had won his laurels in two mining disasters, fell on his neck and wept.

Jack moved down the trench one afternoon to chat with two lance corporals with whom he had struck up an acquaintance. They were fine types, yet totally dissimilar. One was a thick-set man of thirty. In civilian life he was a colliery deputy who was also a studious type and had passed his examinations for under-manager. Quiet, yet confident in his own ability, he gave Jack the surprise of his life when he suggested a game of chess. Jack soon discovered that the deputy knew as much as he did of algebra and Euclid and, though he had not read widely, he had read well.

The other was a younger man. He made no pretence to knowledge but he had a bright, winsome personality which would over-ride most misfortunes. He was also a strong man, with a great deal of energy. They were two of the most useful men in the company, Jack thought and he could not understand why they were still lance corporals. He soon found that they received more than a share of the company's dirty work.

Today, both wore serious faces but they were not rattled. "A bit rough" said Card, the stocky one. "By God it is" said the other, Wharton. "I was just talking to Tommy Smith when I came round the traverse to see what was happening. When I went back, two minutes later, to say something to Tommy, he didn't speak. I looked at him closer. He was as dead as a doornail, sitting there just as before but with a piece of shrapnel through the head".

If anything, the third night was worse. It was dark when an urgent request came for casualty returns. This was Jack's job, of course, but how was it to be done in the dark? It was all very well for Brigade, in their candle-lit dug-outs, to ask for returns but Jack often wondered if they knew how hard it was to carry out their instructions.

"The only thing to do is to hold an oil sheet over a funk hole and light a candle", said the CSM. Dave and he soon obliged. It cannot definitely be stated that the casualty return cost three lives but events strongly suggested it.

The return was safely dispatched to battalion HQ and Jack, Dave and the CSM were crouching in their funk holes when a heavy shell burst right on top of them. Jack felt as if he was suffocating from the acrid fumes. Involuntarily, he began to spring up when he felt the steadying hand of Dave on his arm.

"Steady, son. You are all right". It was the same Dave, always cool, always thinking of the other man and always seeming to know what was required.

Jack's feet were covered in debris and, as the smoke cleared, it was dimly seen that the trench was blocked by a huge wall of earth. Again, Jack had just missed the worst of a shell. From beneath the huge mound came faint moans.

Furiously, the heap was attacked. Only hands could be used for three men were missing. They found them. Two were dead, terribly mutilated. The third, a sergeant, would not live the night.

Next morning, the shelling was not quite so bad and, in the afternoon, the remnants of the company were withdrawn to a support trench. It was a poor trench, only a hundred yards back, yet it was as quiet as the other was rough. There was plenty of accommodation since the company now only numbered 80 men. They were dog-tired and fell asleep like logs. For the time being they had forgotten their hunger and thirst. Time enough to think of that when day dawned.

Next day, however, they could spare no one to fetch in food or drink for L...... was to be attacked in the early afternoon and the battalion was to be held in support, ready for emergencies.

There was some misgiving as the trench was examined in view of possible artillery retaliation. There need have been no fear, however. Not a shell dropped near them despite the heavy bombardment prior to the attack.

The attacking waves went over in fine style. All objectives were carried with slight loss and soon a stream of German prisoners came staggering along the trench. It was at such times that the British Tommy stood out best. Despite the ordeal of the past few days there was nothing but sympathy for the wounded prisoners.

A blond sergeant who was almost carrying a wounded comrade, pleaded for water for the injured man. Fingers to lips he pointed to his stricken comrade. He could not know that Jack and his pals were equally parched. But water bottles were shaken and at last one was found to contain a drop. It was freely given and the look of gratitude fully repaid the sacrifice.

From the unwounded, souvenirs were demanded and it was a lucky prisoner who had a button on his tunic when he had passed through the trench. Rings, too, and all manner of goods changed hands. The Germans didn't seem to mind so long as they escaped with their lives.

Many of the prisoners were fine fellow but a few were mere youths and they looked particularly dejected, even to the extent of fear. Jack wondered what English prisoners looked like and if they would be as well-treated as he knew the Germans would be. Altogether there was quite a string of prisoners; the most Jack's unit had had anything to do with capturing.

Late the next afternoon Jack and Dave were told to clear out to Scots Redoubt, in advance of the rest of the unit. Never had orders been so gladly obeyed. Every man's nerves were at the breaking point. Jack remembered very little of that journey. When at last they got to a road which transport was using they hailed a GS wagon and flung themselves into it without even asking its destination. It was enough for them that it was going down the road. They lay on their backs and yelled and sang for sheer relief. The wagon jolted and banged. The bumps to their heads and tired limbs went unheeded. They shouted the more – anything that came into their heads. It was pure relief.

Fortunately, the wagon passed Scots Redoubt and they alighted. The quartermaster sergeant and the cooks were there. Never before had a reunion been so welcome. Their tale was soon told.

"Well, boys, we must give them a good meal", said the quarter. Soon, kettles were steaming and all was ready when at last the men arrived. Human appetites must be satisfied, even when sorrow is eating at the heart. The most weary of men must put away their sorrow and satisfy the craving for food. Never was meat so delicious.

The skirl of bagpipes awoke Jack next morning. Tears came to his eyes as he watched the kilties of the 15th Division marching past. Nothing equalled bagpipes for preparing men for battle. They looked brave as they swung along, kilts swaying with the rhythm of the march. It was the last time Jack's unit saw the 15th. Their job was to go to R...... but the Warlencourt battles stood between and they were not to be passed that year.

Thus Jack's unit said goodbye to the Somme. Two days later they entrained at Albert station, now brought into use again and they rattled away to Poperinge to begin the longest tour of possibly any unit spent in the Ypres Salient.

CHAPTER 13

It must not be thought that, in the strife and turmoil of the Somme, Jack had banished from his mind the Vision which had meant so much to him on the High Seas, in Egypt and again in France prior to the opening of the fierce fighting in the battle. Very much the reverse. No sooner had he left the trenches on 1 July than he posted off a field card, having carefully crossed out anything that would suggest serious injury. He followed this as soon as possible with a reassuring letter. Lying in bed in Boulogne, he gazed longingly over the sea homewards. He recalled the Hampshire downs where he had taken part in manoeuvres, dwelling on those moors nearer home where she had walked with him

Back on the Somme, he had written often to her, giving no hint of the harassing experiences, rather dwelling more on home scenes and events, seeking by hint and suggestion more news of her. He was consumed by a great longing to see her. Her bright, almost boyish letters lifted him clean out of his surroundings, banishing as if by magic the suffering and agonies about him.

In those long days, made longer by the mental torture, he loved to dream of her, forgetting the whining shells that soared above the trenches; forgetting everything associated with the war. One thing that he could not forget, however, was the impossibility of bridging the gulf that lay between them.

On weary marches, too, when tramp, tramp, hour after hour, they plodded on in dreary rhythm, he loved to daydream. In those dreams he pictured her in summer dress, always cool and fresh, always bright, cheery and sympathetic, always understanding, always sweetly attractive. In those daydreams he took her on wonderful picnics. On hot days they found cosy little wayside inns and consumed tremendous meals – such as rambles love – of eggs and ham.

In rest billets, when other men hurried off to the estaminet to drink their beer or wine, or to listen to the chatter of village girls, his Vision was enough for Jack. All he needed was to be left alone to dream, either in his billet or in a quiet walk by the wayside.

There were times, though, when he dare not think of her. Those times when he crouched in the funk hole, ready for the worst, when shells shrieked and senses were

dulled and wearied by incessant explosions.

Thoughts were too poignant then, for there was nothing to hope for if separation came. There was also the chance that he might be maimed and he could not face the possibility of greeting her, a wreck, ashamed to ask her to take him. There is no worse nightmare for a normal man than the loss of his strength. No one knew what men wrecked in their early years had suffered. To age, it matters less. The mind has become attuned to the gradual weakening. The step is less springy, the eyes are dimmed, hearing is not nearly so acute.

These things come gradually but any one might descend like lightning flash on any one of these thousands of hearty, high-spirited young men; men who used to love to vaunt their strength on the cricket field or in manly stride across hills or moorland. Surely no greater sacrifice could be offered.

Yet the day would come, not many years hence, when this sacrifice of all that youth holds dear would be held as naught by forgetful kinsmen.

Not that any of these men would have expected gratitude. They offered the sacrifice freely and would have spurned gratitude. These were not the men of later years who had had to be cajoled and bribed into taking up arms by promises of lands fit for heroes; or who had needed the eloquent appeal to take up arms to end war for all time. They had heard the call themselves. Their national pride had been touched. They had thought of that little expeditionary force fighting fearful odds and their great spirits had responded as the spirit of any sound lad would respond to the cry of the bully's victim.

Yet the thought of maiming or blinding was ever present in the inmost souls of these young men, not merely for their own sakes but for the sake of those they loved. In their weaker or most tired moments they may have prayed for Blighties; but many a man prayed too that he might be taken altogether to join that youthful company which had already passed over, rather than be broken beyond repair, to face his loved ones as a useless wreck.

In brighter moments, how much his Vision meant to Jack she could never know Had she known what nectar those too-infrequent letters were to a parched soul, she would have written every day. But she could not know. No one at home could know. They doubtless heard disjointed stories of escapes from death but they could not know that these were hourly occurrences, that no man lived a day except by the goodness of the Divine Providence. No man could delude himself for long out here

He might escape a dozen times by his own agility – and an experienced soldier could save his own life often enough – but no one knew better than he that he could not possibly have escaped that dud if it had been a good shell, or could know what prompted him to turn back just as he had been about to enter that doomed bay.

So we hear that, when Jack went rumbling over that poor railway track to the treacherous Salient, he carried his vision with him, to comfort and cheer him through interminable months spent in the mud and blood of Flanders. Away again on the Long, Long Trail, but accompanied still by a beautiful vision of sweet purity and fragrance that would shine as a beacon through the dark clouds about him.

Epilogue

By Stuart Wilson

Readers will have noticed, as a friend of mine commented, this book stops, it does not end. It stops, in fact, with my father barely half way through his war time service.

I feel sure that initially he will have intended to record all of his experiences. However, as the manuscript was not found until many years after his death, there is no way of knowing for certain his original intentions.

In trying to determine why he stopped when he did I found myself wondering why he wrote his story at all. At the end of the War, my father, like so many thousands of others, was left to pick up his life as best he could. No counselling or compensation as applies nowadays but just get on with life. Apparently it was common for them to find great difficulty in talking of their experiences to family, friends and acquaintances and discussions with old comrades was unnecessary. Consequently, the horrific memories were unshared.

I do know that my father visited the battlefields several times in the early 1920's and the style of writing suggests that the book was written at the same time. Perhaps returning to the battlefields and writing the book were my father's way of coping with the memories.

After his first marriage he apparently stopped visiting the battlefields and perhaps that was when he decided to end working on the book. He had a future to live for rather than reliving nightmares.

In 1938, immediately after telling the staff of the Sheffield Independent that the newspaper was to close, he had a chance meeting with an old comrade from the Sheffield City Battalion. The next day, the two of them set off for the Somme again. After that visit he never returned or mentioned the war again.